Wordly Wise

Kenneth Hodkinson

BOOK 7
Revised

Educators Publishing Service, Inc. Cambridge, Mass. 02138

Cover Design/Hugh Price

August 2000 Printing

Educators Publishing Service, Inc.

31 Smith Place, Cambridge, MA 02138-1089

Contents

Word List

(Numbers in parentheses refer to the Word List in which the word appears.)

ABASHED (13)
abdicate (3)
ablution (14)
absolute (25)
abstain (4)
acme (3)
addled (10)
adherent (19)
adulterate (2)
aerie (2)
affirm (16)
affluent (20)
agnostic (28)
alloy (21)
alluring (29)
alto (3)
altruism (26)
ambidextrous (7)
ambivalence (8)
ameliorate (1)
amenable (22)
amity (19)
amnesia (30)
amnesty (28)
amoral (27)
amulet (2)
anarchy (11)
anneal (15)
annuity (17)
apiary (5)
apologist (23)
aqueous (12)
arbiter (13)
arbitrate (29)
arboreal (30)
articulate (3)
ascetic (6)
assonance (24)
assuage (20)
attune (25)
augury (21)
automaton (22)
autonomous (18)
autopsy (9)

avarice (16)

BAUBLE (14)
bayonet (28)
becoming (15)
bedeviled (17)
belligerent (18)
benison (13)
bestial (14)
biannual (23)
bigot (30)
bivouac (4)
bizarre (15)
blatant (7)
bloated (19)
bluff (13)
bombastic (14)
bourgeois (26)
boycott (29)
buoyant (15)
butte (20)
buttress (24)

CADAVER (21)
canker (13)
cant (5)
cartel (27)
cataclysm (19)
cauterize (10)
cede (22)
censer (11)
censor (25)
chary (14)
chaste (12)
chattel (15)
choler (8)
chronometer (23)
collate (29)
collusion (1)
comestible (2)
complacent (20)
complaisant (13)
compunction (9)

conception (24)
condolence (3)
confluence (26)
congenital (14)
congestion (10)
constrain (30)
conundrum (27)
courser (16)
covey (25)
cranium (15)
crass (13)
cremate (7)
criterion (6)
cuisine (14)
culpable (15)
curfew (8)
curtail (4)

DEBUT (9)
deciduous (22)
decorum (17)
decry (21)
defame (13)
default (18)
deficit (26)
defile (11)
definitive (23)
demoralize (12)
demote (14)
depreciate (1)
desiccate (19)
designate (28)
desultory (20)
devise (21)
devotee (16)
diagnose (29)
diatribe (24)
dilemma (27)
dilettante (5)
disconcert (6)
discredit (22)
discreet (23)
discursive (7)
disheveled (19)

disinterested (10)
dismantle (8)
dismember (24)
disparage (22)
disperse (30)
dissertation (20)
divers (17)
dogged (18)
dogmatic (2)
dossier (16)

EFFERVESCE (3)
elective (1)
elemental (17)
emancipate (18)
emote (25)
endorse (15)
ennui (13)
enormity (4)
entail (26)
entourage (11)
entreat (21)
enumerate (27)
enunciate (23)
environs (5)
epaulet (19)
equitable (2)
eradicate (3)
ethnic (24)
euphonious (24)
euthanasia (12)
excavate (28)
exhale (10)
exodus (20)
exonerate (16)
exploit (1)
expository (9)
expound (7)
expunge (11)
extant (17)
extenuating (12)
extinct (22)
extraneous (29)
extremist (23)

extrovert (23)

FACET (3)
facetious (30)
facsimile (1)
faction (6)
fastidious (25)
fathom (8)
fatuous (26)
feign (2)
fiasco (22)
filial (10)
finesse (28)
finite (21)
fissure (4)
floe (25)
flora (18)
florid (23)
fluster (24)
flux (14)
forego (27)
forte (11)
fractious (3)
franchise (16)
freebooter (15)
frowzy (5)
funereal (13)

GALA (12)
gamester (10)
gamut (19)
garb (14)
garner (6)
generic (4)
genre (29)
genteel (20)
genus (30)
germinate (17)
gesticulate (1)
ghastly (28)
ghoul (29)
gibbet (26)
gibe (2)
gird (22)

gist (23)
glutinous (9)
gourmet (18)
granary (5)
graphic (11)
gregarious (12)
grimace (27)
grotesque (3)
grueling (7)
gruesome (24)
guillotine (21)

HALLMARK (15)
hallucination (25)
harangue (10)
hemp (8)
herald (16)
heresy (11)
heterogeneous (17)
hierarchy (26)
hindmost (18)
histrionic (4)
homage (6)
homily (9)
hostelry (30)
humus (27)
hypochondriac (19)

IDEOLOGY (13)
idiom (7)
immutable (25)
impeccable (14)
impediment (5)
imperative (8)
imperial (9)
imperturbable (1)
impious (7)
impolitic (26)
imprecations (6)
impromptu (27)
improvident (4)
inadvertent (28)
incandescent (25)
incapacitate (8)

inception (22)
inclement (12)
incognito (15)
incoherent (5)
indict (6)
indignity (10)
inebriated (20)
inevitable (21)
infatuated (9)
inferno (13)
infidelity (7)
inherent (4)
innovation (8)
inopportune (2)
insidious (11)
instantaneous (16)
instill (9)
interim (19)
intermediary (5)
interpolate (7)
intimate (23)
intrigue (6)
intrinsic (29)
introspective (20)
introvert (4)
invalid (26)
invective (14)
inveterate (8)
invoke (24)
ire (5)
irrational (9)
irrefutable (21)
irrevocable (15)

JETTISON (17)

LACKEY (30)
lancet (6)
largesse (27)
lassitude (25)
legendary (3)
limbo (22)
lionize (1)
lisle (28)

literate (7)
lope (23)
loquacious (2)
luminous (19)
lyrical (29)

MAGNITUDE (8)
maladroit (12)
malcontent (26)
mania (18)
marathon (16)
marauder (9)
martinet (20)
mausoleum (10)
mediate (11)
melodrama (17)
memoirs (18)
mendicant (12)
mercenary (13)
mettle (16)
microcosm (27)
militant (21)
minimum (30)
minion (7)
moral (3)
munificent (25)
munitions (19)

NATURALIST (26)
neo- (4)
nominal (28)
nucleus (29)
nutriment (24)

OBLIGATORY (5)
oblivion (20)
obnoxious (30)
obsolescent (21)
octagon (8)
ocular (17)
ogle (14)
opiate (1)
opulence (18)
ornithologist (10)

outlandish (27)
overwrought (9)

PACIFIC (15)
pacify (22)
paean (2)
palliative (11)
palpitate (23)
panorama (12)
paroxysm (28)
parsimonious (13)
partake (3)
partiality (17)
pasteurize (6)
paucity (1)
pecuniary (24)
pedagogue (19)
pejorative (22)
penury (14)
pernicious (15)
perpetrate (23)
petition (29)
philistine (10)
philtre (4)
pied (25)
pillory (20)
plateau (30)
plebeian (24)
potable (28)
practicable (22)
pragmatic (5)
prate (18)
predicament (16)
prefatory (21)
presentiment (23)
primordial (6)
proclivity (7)
procrastinate (24)
prodigious (11)
progenitor (8)
propaganda (13)
prosaic (19)
provocation (20)
prowess (26)

proxy (4)
psyche (5)
punctilious (6)
punitive (22)

QUADRUPLE (12)
qualm (27)
quandary (9)

RAILLERY (14)
rationalize (10)
rebut (7)
recapitulate (2)
recession (17)
recluse (21)
recourse (4)
redoubtable (11)
regale (19)
relegate (3)
replete (12)
requite (23)
residue (18)
resilient (8)
reticent (9)
retinue (15)
retrogress (13)
retrospective (25)
revelry (5)
revoke (20)
roué (24)
russet (26)

SABOTAGE (6)
salutary (10)
sanctimonious (16)
sanction (29)
scapegoat (4)
scathing (1)
scenario (30)
scintillate (14)
scrip (15)
scuttle (2)
secular (27)
sedition (25)

Introduction

This book has four main purposes: (1) to familiarize you with a large number of words (about 500) that you are likely to encounter in your reading or in various achievement tests designed to measure the extent of your vocabulary, (2) to give you a knowledge of how words are formed and how they are used, (3) to increase your ability to perform well on various kinds of vocabulary tests (entrance to college and to many occupations depends to a large extent on a person's demonstrated ability in this area), and (4) to accomplish the above in a way that you will find interesting, even enjoyable.

Each of the thirty lessons in this book has three exercises. Exercise A is designed to give you a firm grasp of the meaning or meanings of the words on the Word List. Exercise B is designed to make you familiar with how these words may and may not be used in sentences. These two exercises are the same throughout the book; Exercise C varies from lesson to lesson. Be sure to read carefully the instruction for each one.

Following each lesson is a Wordly Wise section which discusses the origin and formation of words, distinguishes between words commonly confused, provides a guide to pronunciation where needed, and generally deals with any points that may need clarification.

At the end of every third lesson there is a review of all the words in those lessons plus some review words. This is in the form of a crossword puzzle in which the clues are definitions of the words that have been studied. In order to get the most enjoyment out of these puzzles, come adequately prepared with a sure knowledge of the words covered.

Before beginning the first lesson, study the terms defined below. Refer back to this page if you encounter any of these terms and are unsure of their meanings.

Etymology is the science that studies the origins and histories of words; it is also the name given to the history of a word which shows where it came from and how it changed into its present form and meaning.

A *root* is a word or part of a word that is used as a base for making other words. The word *move* is the root of such words as *remove* and *movement*.

A *prefix* is a syllable or group of syllables joined to the beginning of a word to change its meaning. Some common prefixes are *un-, non-, anti,* and *in-.* In the word *remove, re-* is a prefix.

A *suffix* is a syllable or group of syllables added to the end of a word to change its meaning. Some common suffixes are *-able, -ary, -ful,* and *-tion.* In the word *movement, -ment* is a suffix.

A *synonym* is a word having the same or nearly the same meaning as another word in the same language. The English *cheese* has the same meaning as the French *fromage,* but they are not synonyms. *Little* and *small* are synonyms; so are *valiant* and *brave.*

An *antonym* is a word that is opposite in meaning to another word. *Strong* and *weak* are antonyms; so are *up* and *down.*

A *homonym* is a word that is pronounced the same as another word but has a different meaning and usually a different spelling. *Hoarse* and *horse* are homonyms; so are *bow* and *bough.*

An *analogy* is a similarity in some respect between two things; it is also a comparing of something with something else. Word relationship tests make use of analogy in the following way. A pair of words is given and the relationship between them must be established. The third word must then be matched with one of a number of choices (usually four or five) to express the same kind of relationship. Here is an example:

ant is to *insect* as *robin* is to which of the following
(1) fly (2) nest (3) bird (4) sing (5) wing

The relationship between the first pair, *ant* and *insect*, is one of class; ants belong to the class of living things called insects. By selecting choice (3), we express the same kind of relationship since robins belong to the class of living things called birds. The form in which analogy questions are usually put together with the correct answer is shown here:

ant:insect :: robin:
(1) fly (2) nest (3) bird (4) sing (5) wing

Note that balance must be maintained between each pair of words. If we go from *ant* to *insect* on one side, we cannot go from *bird* to *robin* on the other for the relationship between the two pairs would not then be identical. The parts of speech of each of the two pairs must also match; *noun:verb* must be followed by *noun:verb*, *noun:adjective* by *noun:adjective* and so on.

In addition to the example given, there are many other possible relationships between words. Here are some of the more common ones:

(1) synonyms (sad:gloomy)
(2) antonyms (true:false)
(3) homonyms (rough:ruff)
(4) part:whole (page:book)
(5) worker:tool (painter:brush)
(6) worker:article produced (poet:poem)
(7) function (knife:cut)
(8) symbol (dove:peace)
(9) description (circle:round)
(10) size (twig:branch)
(11) lack (invalid:health)
(12) cause (germ:disease)
(13) sex (bull:cow)
(14) parent:child (mother:daughter)
(15) noun:adjective (warmth:warm)
(16) type:characteristic (cow:herbivorous)

A *metaphor* is a figure of speech in which a term or phrase is applied to something to which it is not literally applicable in order to show a likeness. The exclamation "What a pig!" would refer to a greedy person if meant metaphorically; it would refer to the animal raised for its pork and bacon if meant literally. Metaphor extends the meanings of words; *pig* has acquired its secondary meaning, "a greedy or filthy person," in this way.

To *denote* is to provide with a factual, exact definition. The word *mother* denotes a female parent. To *connote* is to suggest some feeling or idea in addition to the actual meaning. The word *mother*, to most people, connotes love, care, warmth, and tenderness.

Chapter One

Word List 1

AMELIORATE	GESTICULATE	SPECIES
COLLUSION	IMPERTURBABLE	STIPEND
DEPRECIATE	LIONIZE	ULTERIOR
ELECTIVE	OPIATE	VAINGLORIOUS
EXPLOIT	PAUCITY	WIZENED
FACSIMILE	SCATHING	

Look up the words above in your dictionary. Note that many of them have more than one meaning. When you think that you know *all* the meanings of *all* the words, go on to the exercise below.

EXERCISE 1A

From the four choices following each phrase or sentence, you are to circle the letter preceding the one that is closest in meaning to the italicized word. Where the same word appears more than once, you should note that it is being used in different senses.

1. to *ameliorate* the conditions
   (a) discuss (b) improve (c) ignore (d) worsen

2. working in *collusion*
   (a) great danger (b) complete ignorance (c) secret agreement (d) alternating shifts

3. How much did it *depreciate*?
   (a) sell for (b) gain in value (c) cost (d) lose in value

4. to *depreciate* someone
   (a) suggest (b) congratulate (c) fire (d) belittle

5. *elective* officials
   (a) unpaid (b) appointed by the president (c) chosen by vote (d) serving for life

6. *elective* subjects
   (a) advanced (b) elementary (c) optional (d) required

7. to *exploit* the wealth of the sea
   (a) be ignorant of (b) make an investigation of (c) make full use of (d) measure

8. to *exploit* a person
   (a) reveal information about (b) take unfair advantage of (c) examine the background of (d) follow closely behind

9. news of the *exploit*
   (a) small explosion (b) daring deed (c) discovery (d) defeat

10. a *facsimile* of a book
    (a) exact copy (b) record of sales (c) loose cover (d) revised edition

11. to *gesticulate* at someone
    (a) express displeasure (b) hurl defiance (c) wave one's arms (d) look scornfully

12. an *imperturbable* person
    (a) discouraged (b) calm (c) impressed (d) annoyed

13. to *lionize* someone
    (a) go in fear of (b) hold in contempt (c) have control over (d) hold in great esteem

14. to administer an *opiate*
    (a) severe beating (b) soothing drug (c) strong rebuke (d) course of treatment

15. a *paucity* of talent
    (a) scarcity (b) wealth (c) neglect (d) channeling

16. a *scathing* reply
    (a) mildly encouraging (b) boldly challenging (c) gently scolding (d) bitingly severe

17. many *species*
    (a) small streams joining a larger (b) kinds of plants and animals (c) types of layered rocks (d) false reasons or excuses

18. a small *stipend*
    (a) debt (b) salary (c) favor (d) increase

19. *ulterior* motives
    (a) generous (b) obvious (c) carefully considered (d) hidden

20. an *ulterior* event
(a) unrecorded (b) future (c) insignificant
(d) past

21. a *vainglorious* person
(a) boastful (b) noble (c) unknown
(d) popular

22. a *wizened* face
(a) oily (b) pale (c) intelligent (d) wrinkled

Check your answers against the correct ones given below. The answers are not in order; this is to prevent your eye from catching sight of the correct answers before you have had a chance to do the exercise on your own.

9b. 22d. 14b. 10a. 19d. 18b. 6c. 3d. 17b. 4d. 1b. 20b. 5c. 8b. 12b. 16d. 11c. 7c. 15a. 2c. 21a. 13d.

Look up in your dictionary all the words for which you gave incorrect answers. Only when you have done this should you go on to the next exercise.

EXERCISE 1B

Each word in Word List 1 is used several times in the sentences below to illustrate different meanings or usage. One of the sentences for each word uses the italicized word incorrectly. You are to circle the letter preceding the sentence.

1. (a) She was quite ill for a while but is now *ameliorating*. (b) Attempts are being made to *ameliorate* the conditions of the slums. (c) The situation will *ameliorate* with time.

2. (a) It seems that the store manager worked in *collusion* with the two thieves. (b) The president made a plea for closer *collusion* among the various departments. (c) Someone on the general's staff had been acting in *collusion* with the enemy.

3. (a) Many of our critics have a tendency to *depreciate* the writings of modern authors. (b) The car is bound to *depreciate* in value as it gets older. (c) Although I *depreciated* your kind offer, I was not able to take advantage of it. (d) If you *depreciate* yourself, others will take you at your own valuation.

4. (a) All students must take English, but art and music are *electives*. (b) Federal judgeships are filled by appointment and are not *elective*. (c) The candidate appealed to the *electives* to return him to office for a third term.

5. (a) When we have *exploited* all the logs in the woodshed, we shall have to chop more. (b) He entertained us with an account of his *exploits* in the war. (c) We have not yet begun to *exploit* the mineral wealth of the region. (d) Talented children are sometimes *exploited* by their parents.

6. (a) This shop sells *facsimiles* of famous paintings at very low prices. (b) The two pictures are *facsimile* in every respect. (c) The publisher is bringing out a *facsimile* edition of Doctor Johnson's dictionary.

7. (a) Despite our frantic *gesticulations*, the waitress continued to ignore us. (b) He *gesticulated* across the room to us as a signal for us to follow him. (c) A large snake sometimes takes several days to *gesticulate* a meal.

8. (a) Her *imperturbability* had a calming effect on the other passengers. (b) The *imperturbable* waters of the lake indicated fair weather. (c) The job requires an *imperturbable* person who won't panic in a crisis.

9. (a) Celebrities such as movie stars are *lionized* for a few years, then quickly forgotten. (b) The animal trainer, after years spent with lions, was completely *lionized*.

10. (a) Our teacher complained that television has become an *opiate* of the people. (b) After swallowing the *opiate*, she fell into a prolonged stupor. (c) Morphine and other *opiates* are being smuggled into the country. (d) There were fields of *opiate* growing in the valley, ready to be harvested.

11. (a) The food was so *paucity* that we were still hungry at the end of the meal. (b) The choir suffers from a *paucity* of good male voices.

12. (a) The principal administered a *scathing* rebuke to the two bullies. (b) She gave the students who had cheated a *scathing* that they never forgot. (c) The book contains a *scathing* attack on his country's foreign policy.

13. (a) There is a *species* of student that seems not to want to graduate from college. (b) The lion and the tiger belong to different *species* of the cat family. (c) In the next cage were a pair of *species* from South America.

14. (a) The woman gave him a *stipend* of ten dollars for finding her lost dog. (b) For performing these duties, you will receive a *stipend* of fifty dollars a week. (c) The scholarship carries with it a *stipend* sufficient for living expenses. (d) A pensioner's *stipend* is often barely sufficient for him or her to live on.

15. (a) I suspect that he has an *ulterior* motive for his request. (b) There are reasons, both immediate and *ulterior*, for our supporting this venture. (c) The *ulterior* of the car looked a little the worse for wear.

16. (a) She was a *vainglorious* and arrogant woman, full of her own importance. (b) It was one of those *vainglorious* days in the fall when the leaves are turning.

17. (a) She suggested that we should be *wizened* as to what was going on. (b) The apples we had stored were so *wizened* that we threw them out. (c) His face was so *wizened* that I believed him when he said he was ninety years old.

EXERCISE 1C

Complete the following sentences by filling in the appropriate form of either the verb *denote* or the verb *connote*. These two terms are explained in the Introduction.

1. One way to show what a concrete noun . . . . is to point to the object it stands for.

2. Abstract nouns like *justice* and *freedom* . . . . different things to different people.

3. The word *home* . . . . comfort and security in the minds of most people.

4. The word *biped* . . . . a two-legged animal.

5. The prefix *mono-* may. . . . . "one" or "single."

6. The word *home* . . . . a house, together with its grounds, fittings, and furnishings, and occupied by a family.

7. Although pigs are actually clean animals, the word *pig* . . . . filth in the minds of many people.

9. The word *horse* . . . . a large, solid-hoofed, herbivorous mammal domesticated by humans and used as a beast of burden.

WORDLY WISE 1

DEPRECIATE means "to belittle" or "to lessen the value of." (Countries dislike having to *depreciate* their currencies. Do not *depreciate* the value of your own contribution.) *Deprecate* means "to express disapproval of, usually regretfully." (He *deprecates* the practice of arguing without having all the facts.)

To GESTICULATE is to use a series of *gestures*, especially in conversation, or to make a single gesture in an excited or animated manner. A *gesture* is a single act of *gesticulation*.

SPECIES is spelled the same in both singular and plural (a *species*; several *species*). *Specie* (without the final *s*) is a quite different word and means "money in the form of coin."

Etymology

(See the Introduction for an explanation of this term, together with the notes on roots, prefixes, and suffixes.)

Study the roots given below, together with the English words derived from them. Capitalized words are those given in the Word List. You should look up in a dictionary any words that are unfamiliar to you.

Roots: *fac, fec* (make) Latin — Examples: *FAC*SIMILE, *fac*tory, per*fec*t

simil (like) Latin—Example: FAC*SIMIL*E

leg, lic, lect (choose) Latin — Examples: E*LECT*IVE, se*lect*, e*lect*ion

---

Word List 2

ADULTERATE	FEIGN	SCUTTLE
AERIE	GIBE	STALEMATE
AMULET	INOPPORTUNE	STRATEGIC
COMESTIBLE	LOQUACIOUS	ULTIMATUM
DOGMATIC	PAEAN	VEGETATE
EQUITABLE	RECAPITULATE	

Look up the words above in your dictionary. Note that many of them have more than one meaning. When you think that you know *all* the meanings of *all* the words, go on to the exercise below.

EXERCISE 2A

From the four choices following each phrase or sentence, you are to circle the letter preceding the one that is closest in meaning to the italicized word. Where the same word appears more than once, you should note that it is being used in different senses.

1. to *adulterate* the food
   (a) preserve by salting (b) chew thoroughly (c) season heavily (d) make impure

2. the eagle's *aerie*
   (a) claw (b) beak (c) nest (d) victim

3. a wooden *amulet*
   (a) charm (b) support (c) cart (d) platter

4. a supply of *comestibles*
   (a) tools (b) fuel (c) ammunition (d) food

5. *dogmatic* opinions
   (a) so obviously untrue as to be laughable (b) changing frequently (c) asserted strongly but without proof (d) supported by evidence

6. an *equitable* arrangement
   (a) artistic (b) fair (c) secret (d) generous

7. to *feign* illness
   (a) avoid (b) suffer (c) pretend (d) fear

8. to *gibe* at someone
   (a) smile (b) glance sideways (c) hurl blows (d) sneer

9. an *inopportune* moment
   (a) unhappy (b) fleeting (c) dreaded (d) unsuitable

10. a *loquacious* person
    (a) talkative (b) attractive (c) friendly (d) mysterious

11. a *paean* to liberty
    (a) fatal blow (b) song of praise (c) first move (d) severe setback

12. to *recapitulate* what happened
    (a) remember vividly (b) live over again (c) restate briefly (d) make a careful record of

13. to fill the *scuttle*
    (a) drinking cup (b) coal bucket (c) wine barrel (d) storage box

14. to *scuttle* across the floor
    (a) leap gracefully (b) roll noisily (c) move quickly (d) slide smoothly

15. to *scuttle* the ship
    (a) refuel in mid ocean (b) sink deliberately (c) haul onto dry land (d) overhaul

16. to reach a *stalemate*
    (a) decision (b) deadlock (c) agreement (d) verdict

17. *strategic* aims

(a) to do with educational policy (b) to do with personal ambition (c) to do with recreational pursuits (d) to do with military planning

18. presented with an *ultimatum*
    (a) difficult choice (b) token of thanks (c) final demand (d) complex problem

19. no desire to *vegetate*
    (a) think deeply (b) grow vegetables (c) live in the country (d) lead a dull life

Check your answers against the correct ones given below. The answers are not in order; this is to prevent your eye from catching sight of the correct answers before you have had a chance to do the exercise on your own.

4d. 16b. 10a. 14c. 7c. 11b. 18c. 6b. 2c. 12c. 1d. 19d. 15b. 9d. 17d. 8d. 13b. 3a. 5c.

Look up in your dictionary all the words for which you gave incorrect answers. Only when you have done this should you go on to the next exercise.

EXERCISE 2B

Each word in Word List 2 is used several times in the sentences below to illustrate different meanings or usage. One of the sentences for each word uses the italicized word incorrectly. You are to circle the letter preceding the sentence.

1. (a) The children had *adulterated* the rug by walking over it with their muddy boots. (b) The dairy owner was found guilty of *adulterating* the milk by adding water to it. (c) The *adulterated* meat products were ordered destroyed by city food inspectors.

2. (a) Birds of prey build their *aeries* in high, inaccessible mountain places. (b) An *aerie* sound came from the darkness.

3. (a) The people wore *amulets* around their necks to ward off evil spirits. (b) The natives danced an *amulet* before battle, in the belief that it would bring victory. (c) The *amulets* were worn as much for ornament as for protection.

4. (a) They bought loaves of bread, meat, and other *comestibles*. (b) A fine assortment of *comestibles* filled the tables. (c) Gasoline vapors and air make a highly *comestible* combination.

5. (a) He insisted *dogmatically* that the sun revolves around the earth. (b) When I questioned her, she smiled *dogmatically* and refused to answer. (c) He has made a close study of the *dogmatic* writings of the early fathers of the church. (d) It is useless to discuss anything with such a *dogmatic* person.

6. (a) It is difficult to remain *equitable* while walking across a tightrope. (b) The proceeds will be shared *equitably* among the three groups. (c) The party is pressing for more *equitable* tax laws.

7. (a) The opossum sometimes escapes from an attacker by *feigning* death. (b) They showered the emperor with *feigned* compliments. (c) She *feigned* an excuse for not going with them. (d) "I would *feign* go with you," said the minstrel to the queen.

8. (a) Her friends *gibed* her for her cowardice. (b) The boy's parents urged him to ignore the cruel *gibes* of the other children. (c) They dropped the mainsail and used only the *gibe* because of the strong wind.

9. (a) Patients telephone the doctor at the most *inopportune* moments. (b) "Shorty" is a most *inopportune* name for a star basketball player. (c) You have chosen a most *inopportune* time to call, because I was just going to bed.

10. (a) With a *loquacious* wave of her hand, she signaled for us to be seated. (b) He is not a *loquacious* person, but tonight he was unusually talkative. (c) The *loquaciousness* of her mother-in-law was a sore point with her.

(d) The death scene is made absurd by the *loquacity* of the dying man.

11. (a) Mexican *paeans* toiled long hours in the fields for a few pesos a day. (b) Their voices rose in a *paean* of praise to the god Apollo. (c) The crowd roared in a wild *paean* of joy.

12. (a) Allow me to *recapitulate* the situation as I see it. (b) After suffering repeated attacks, the town was forced to *recapitulate*. (c) Before each episode the narrator *recapitulates* everything that has happened so far.

13. (a) Rather than allow the ship to be seized by the enemy, the captain *scuttled* it. (b) The sudden failure of the business *scuttled* our plans for an early retirement. (c) A bomb from an enemy plane struck the ship's magazine and *scuttled* it. (d) As I opened the door, I saw something furry *scuttle* under the sofa.

14. (a) A chess game ends in a *stalemate* when the king's only move puts it in check. (b) Discussions went on for so long that they grew *stalemate*. (c) If discussions reach a *stalemate*, they will be broken off.

15. (a) The hydrogen bomb is a *strategic* weapon that cannot be used for tactical purposes. (b) The Hawaiian Islands are of great *strategic* importance to the United States. (c) By means of a clever *strategic*, she made off with most of their money. (d) The generals work out *strategic* plans and leave tactical operations to the junior officers.

16. (a) If our country's *ultimatum* is ignored, war will be only a matter of hours away. (b) Germany tried to *ultimatum* France into surrendering before a shot had been fired. (c) Her landlady issued an *ultimatum* that she get rid of the dog or leave the house.

17. (a) His only interest is *vegetating* his garden and taking long walks. (b) She's afraid that she will just *vegetate* if she retires from business.

EXERCISE 2C

In each of the sentences below a word has been omitted. From the four words provided, select the one that best completes the sentence. Allow ten minutes for this test. If you cannot answer a question, go on to the next without delay. If you have time left over at the end, go back and try to fill in unanswered questions.

14 or over correct:	excellent
11 to 13 correct:	good
10 or under correct:	thorough review of **A** exercises indicated

1. He did what he could to .... working conditions in the factory.
   adulterate recapitulate ameliorate stalemate

2. She received a(n) .... of two thousand dollars a year.
   paean comestible amulet stipend

3. If they ignore our ...., we will be forced to declare war.
   ultimatum elective facsimile recapitulation

4. The captain .... his ship to prevent its falling into enemy hands.
   exploited depreciated feigned scuttled

5. She .... her workers by paying very low wages.
   ameliorates exploits vegetates recapitulates

6. Discussions reached a(n) ....
   and were broken off.
   collusion ultimatum stalemate paucity

7. Allow me to .... the main points of my argument.
   recapitulate adulterate ameliorate gesticulate

8. The .... were packed in the picnic hamper.
   comestibles paeans species exploits

6

9. "I'm right and you're wrong," he asserted
. . . .
loquaciously dogmatically strategically
electively

10. You picked a most . . . .
moment to ask for my help.
imperturbable inopportune ulterior elective

11. The eagle's . . . . is located
high in the mountains.
aerie amulet paean facsimile

12. Amelia Earhart's most publicized . . . .
was her attempt to fly around the world.
facsimile recapitulation paean exploit

13. The crowds . . . . the player
who had led the team to victory.
lionized gesticulated recapitulated
ameliorated

14. The actors were very upset when they read the
. . . . review of the play.
elective ulterior strategic scathing

15. We are just beginning to . . . . the
mineral wealth of the ocean.
depreciate exploit feign vegetate

WORDLY WISE 2

AERIE is sometimes spelled *eyrie*; the former is more usual, but both are correct.

GIBE, meaning "to taunt," may also be spelled *jibe*. *Gibe* has just this one meaning, but *jibe*, in addition to being the alternative spelling of *gibe*, has two other meanings, (1) "to change course suddenly while sailing," and (2) "to be in agreement; to fit."

STRATEGIC and *tactical* are words sometimes confused. Both are primarily military terms that have come to have nonmilitary applications. *Strategic* refers to overall planning on a large scale; *tactical* refers to the actual process of moving or handling military forces. (*Strategy* is usually worked out by the generals and other senior officers; *tactics* are usually left to the junior officers in the field.)

Since *capitulate* means "to surrender," one might expect RECAPITULATE to mean "to surrender again." It does *not* mean this. It means "to restate; to sum up."

Etymology

Study the roots and prefixes given below, together with the English words derived from them. Capitalized words are those given in the Word List. You should look up in a dictionary any words that are unfamiliar to you.

Prefixes: *re-* (back) Latin – Examples: *RE-CAPITULATE*, *re*turn, *re*fund
re- (again) Latin – Examples: *re*decorate, *re*tell, *re*make

Root: *equa* or *equi* (equal) Latin – Examples: *EQUI*TABLE, *equa*tion, *equa*lity
aqua (water) Latin – Examples: *aqua*tic, *aqua*duct, *aqua*rium

Word List 3

ABDICATE	FACET	RELEGATE
ACME	FRACTIOUS	SLAPSTICK
ALTO	GROTESQUE	STATUTORY
ARTICULATE	LEGENDARY	TURNKEY
CONDOLENCE	MORAL	UNTENABLE
EFFERVESCE	PARTAKE	WAFT
ERADICATE		

Look up the words above in your dictionary. Note that many of them have more than one meaning. When you think that you know *all* the meanings of *all* the words, go on to the following exercise.

EXERCISE 3A

From the four choices following each phrase or sentence, you are to circle the letter preceding the one that is closest in meaning to the italicized word. Where the same word appears more than once, you should note that it is being used in different senses.

1. to *abdicate* a responsibility
(a) assume (b) deny (c) relinquish (d) seek

2. the *acme* of one's career
(a) low point (b) end (c) high point (d) start

3. a fine *alto*
   (a) player of a stringed instrument (b) person singing second highest part in four-part harmony (c) actor who performs without words (d) formal speech given without notes

4. an *articulate* statement
   (a) disjointed (b) defiant (c) apologetic (d) clearly spoken

5. an *articulated* dummy
   (a) talking (b) life-size (c) jointed (d) carved

6. a letter of *condolence*
   (a) congratulation (b) sympathy (c) thanks (d) credit

7. to begin to *effervesce*
   (a) turn cloudy (b) give off fumes (c) turn into a gas (d) give off bubbles

8. an *effervescent* personality
   (a) withdrawn (b) changeable (c) dull (d) lively

9. to *eradicate* a nuisance
   (a) put up with (b) complain about (c) get rid of (d) be annoyed by

10. the *facets* of gems
    (a) settings (b) flashing lights (c) changing colors (d) polished sides

11. a *fractious* child
    (a) unruly (b) sickly (c) intelligent (d) obedient

12. *grotesque* drawings
    (a) carefully executed (b) very detailed (c) wildly distorted (d) charmingly simple

13. a *legendary* hero
    (a) awarded many medals (b) of Greek or Roman times (c) once popular, now forgotten (d) famous in story

14. high *morals*
    (a) achievements (b) supporting structures (c) taxes on property (d) standards of behavior

15. *moral* support
    (a) with unspoken reservations (b) of a whole nation (c) spiritual rather than physical (d) too little and too late

16. a story with a *moral*
    (a) vague and indefinite ending (b) lesson to be learned (c) surprise ending (d) strong narrative plot

17. a *moral* question
    (a) having to do with the law (b) having an answer which is already known (c) having to do with right and wrong (d) having no answer

18. to *partake* of the food
    (a) decline an offering (b) eat one's share (c) make a tasteful display (d) object to the price or quality

19. *relegated* to the minor leagues
    (a) dropped (b) restricted (c) invited (d) offered

20. to *relegate* duties
    (a) assume (b) neglect (c) perform (d) assign

21. to employ *slapstick*
    (a) sly tricks (b) a style of fighting with wooden staves (c) heavy-duty glue (d) crude comedy

22. *statutory* requirements
    (a) unchanging (b) fixed by law (c) that may be disregarded (d) extremely strict

23. a grim *turnkey*
    (a) prison cell (b) judge (c) jailer (d) prison sentence

24. an *untenable* position
    (a) strong (b) exposed (c) uncomfortable (d) indefensible

25. to *waft* through the window
    (a) gesticulate (b) enter secretively (c) call

softly (d) be carried by air

Check your answers against the correct ones given below. The answers are not in order; this is to prevent your eye from catching sight of the correct answers before you have had a chance to do the exercise on your own.

9c. 22b. 14d. 10d. 19a. 18b. 6b. 24d. 3b. 17c. 4d. 23c. 1c. 20d. 5c. 8d. 12c. 16b. 11a. 7d. 15c. 2c. 25d. 21d. 13d.

Look up in your dictionary all the words for which you gave incorrect answers. Only when you have done this should you go on to the next exercise.

EXERCISE 3B

Each word in Word List 3 is used several times in the sentences below to illustrate different meanings or usage. One of the sentences for each word uses the italicized word incorrectly. You are to circle the letter preceding the sentence.

1. (a) This country cannot easily *abdicate* its overseas responsibilities. (b) King Edward VIII assumed the title Duke of Windsor following his *abdication*. (c) I *abdicated* myself to the fact that we were not going to win the contest.

2. (a) Britain reached the *acme* of its power at the end of the nineteenth century. (b) From the *acme* of the mountain we could see for miles around. (c) This new model represents the very *acme* of perfection.

3. (a) The viola is the *alto* of the violin family. (b) When he reached adolescence, his voice began to *alto*. (c) Her voice was too high for an *alto*, so she sang soprano.

4. (a) I admired the *articulate* craftsmanship of the carving. (b) The French teacher carefully *articulated* every sound. (c) The limbs of the dummy are *articulated* so that it can assume various positions. (d) She is a very *articulate*

speaker and is expected to win the inter-school debate.

5. (a) The parents of the dead soldier received a letter of *condolence* from the president. (b) She *condolenced* herself with the thought that she was at least healthy. (c) Please accept my *condolences*.

6. (a) The soda water *effervesces* because of the escaping carbon dioxide. (b) The garden had been sadly neglected, and weeds *effervesced* everywhere. (c) His *effervescent* manner helped to enliven the dinner party.

7. (a) She claims that crime will never be *eradicated* as long as there is poverty. (b) The weeds are so deeply rooted that they are difficult to *eradicate*. (c) Roads *eradicate* out in every direction from the center of the town.

8. (a) He gave her a *facet*-shaped diamond worth one thousand dollars. (b) There are many *facets* to her personality. (c) He showed me a many *faceted* diamond. (d) She has an intimate knowledge of every *facet* of the business.

9. (a) The *fractiousness* of the crew at times bordered on mutiny. (b) The doctor decided that the bone was not *fractious* and did not need a cast. (c) The children are *fractious* because they are tired and hungry.

10. (a) He twisted his face into the most *grotesque* expressions. (b) The newspapers *grotesqued* my remarks so much they were barely recognizable. (c) Her attempts to imitate the manners of the aristocracy were a *grotesque* caricature.

11. (a) Her story sounded true, but I suspected that it was *legendary*. (b) The *legendary* city of Atlantis excites the curiosity of many people. (c) His exploits as a World War I air ace are *legendary*. (d) The story concerns that *legendary* figure Annie Oakley.

12. (a) The 24-0 defeat caused the team's *moral*

to sink even lower. (b) The *moral* of the story is that the more people have, the more they want. (c) He is an extremely *moral* person, always concerned about doing what is right. (d) The courts are concerned with legal issues and not with *moral* questions.

13. (a) He *partook* of the food we had brought and offered to pay us for it. (b) You may not *partake* what is not rightfully yours. (c) All people desire to *partake* of the good life that is available in this country.

14. (a) The sofa with the broken spring was *relegated* to the attic. (b) The team finishing last is *relegated* to a lower league. (c) The *relegates* voted overwhelmingly in favor of the resolution. (d) The detailed work was *relegated* to committees set up for the purpose.

15. (a) She dislikes *slapstick* comedy, preferring something more sophisticated. (b) The comedian *slapsticked* the audience with a series of crude jokes. (c) We soon tired of the pies thrown in people's faces and the rest of the *slapstick*.

16. (a) The factory closes down on all *statutory* holidays. (b) If your entry into the country was not *statutory*, you are liable to be deported. (c) Sixty-five is the *statutory* retiring age.

17. (a) The colors are *turnkeyed* to each other in a most pleasing manner. (b) By bribing the *turnkey*, the prisoners obtained better food while in jail.

18. (a) Her argument was so *untenable* that she quickly abandoned it. (b) Your claim that you suffered injuries is quite *untenable*. (c) The bar gets so hot that it is *untenable* unless you wear gloves.

19. (a) Every warp and *waft* in the carpet was spun by hand. (b) A strong *waft* of ammonia assailed my nostrils when I opened the bottle.

(c) The appetizing smell of frying bacon came *wafting* in from the kitchen. (d) The faint sounds of the band playing in the park came *wafting* through the trees.

EXERCISE 3C

This exercise is designed to enable you to find out how quickly and accurately you can handle questions dealing with synonyms. (An explanation of synonyms is given in the Introduction.) It also tests how well you have learned the vocabulary words covered so far.

Underline the word that is most similar in meaning to the CAPITALIZED word. Allow only ten minutes for this test. If you cannot answer a question, go on to the next one without delay. If you have time left over at the end, go back and try to fill in unanswered questions.

22 or over correct:	excellent
17 to 21 correct:	good
16 or under correct:	thorough review of A exercises indicated

1. BANISH
   ameliorate exploit relegate adulterate partake

2. CALM
   imperturbable stalemate ulterior aerie condolence

3. DRUG
   amulet stipend acme opiate paean

4. SCARCITY
   opiate stalemate stipend statutory paucity

5. HIDDEN
   strategic ulterior fractious elective inopportune

6. FLOAT
   partake waft gibe scuttle feign

7. CHARM
   facet paean comestible amulet opiate

8. MOCK

   paean gibe ameliorate vainglorious exploit

9. CLASS

   stipend species opiate elective facet

10. RESIGN

    ameliorate gesticulate lionize abdicate exploit

11. PEAK

    moral acme amulet alto paean

12. PRONOUNCE

    articulate gesticulate depreciate adulterate feign

13. SYMPATHY

    paean opiate stalemate condolence gibe

14. BUBBLE

    facet effervesce ameliorate recapitulate comestible

15. REMOVE

    eradicate scuttle gibe exploit depreciate

16. FACE

    alto turnkey lionize paean facet

17. DISTORTED

    ulterior grotesque wizened loquacious dogmatic

18. PEEVISH

    vainglorious loquacious effervesce fractious slapstick

19. EATABLE

    tenable comestible equitable adulterate loquacious

20. FAIR

    untenable legendary aerie equitable dogmatic

21. PRETEND

    lionize adulterate feign vegetate gesticulate

22. TALKATIVE

    vainglorious elective comestible fractious loquacious

23. IMPROVE

    depreciate stipend partake ameliorate scuttle

24. BELITTLE

    exploit depreciate feign vegetate articulate

25. COPY

    articulate paean relegate eradicate facsimile

WORDLY WISE 3

LEGENDARY is an adjective meaning "famed in story or legend." A *legendry* (without the *a*) is a collection of stories or legends. It is a noun.

MORAL (pronounced *MOR- əl*) is an adjective and means "concerned with right conduct or with matters of right and wrong." *Morale* (pronounced *mo-RAL*) is a noun and means "a mental state or attitude, particularly one of well-being." (*Note:* the symbol ə indicates the pronunciation of the letter *a* in *about* and *ago*.)

Etymology

Study the roots and prefixes given below, together with the English words derived from them. Capitalized words are those given in the Word List. You should look up in a dictionary any words that are unfamiliar to you.

Prefixes: *con-* (with) Latin — Examples: *CON*DOLENCE, *con*tact, *con*duct
com- (with) Latin — Examples: *com*ply, *com*pete

Roots: *radi(c)* (root) Latin — Examples: *ERADIC*ATE, *radi*sh, *radic*al
radi (ray or spoke) Latin — Examples: *radi*us, *radi*ate
dole or *dolo* (grieve) Latin — Examples: CON*DOLE*NCE, *dolo*rous, *dole*ful

The crossword puzzle for this first chapter has 53 clues. Each clue is a definition of a word from Word Lists 1, 2, or 3. Unless otherwise stated, a word is always used in the form in which it appears on the Word List; each word is used only once.

For every crossword puzzle after this one, review words are included. These are indicated by the number of the Word List from which they are taken appearing after the clue.

ACROSS

1. to lead a dull, inactive life
4. an exact reproduction or copy
7. to be borne lightly through the air
9. remaining calm under trying conditions
11. an insufficient number or amount
13. to make arm or hand movements
15. happening at the wrong time
19. looking strange and unreal because distorted
20. a jailer
21. to put in a less important position
22. crude comedy marked by horseplay
23. a drug containing some form of opium
24. to share in the eating or drinking of
27. to make or become less unpleasant
28. fixed by rule or law
32. the range of the second highest part in four-part harmony
33. to sink (a ship one is on) deliberately
35. a secret agreement for a wrong purpose
38. a regular, fixed payment, as a salary
40. very talkative
41. to root out; to remove
43. having to do with right and wrong
45. to give up formally; to relinquish
46. a song of joy or praise
47. to treat as a celebrity
48. to give off bubbles of gas
49. too positive or arrogant in stating opinions

DOWN

1. showing excessive vanity
2. chosen by vote rather than by appointment
3. to express sounds clearly and distinctly
4. ill-tempered and unruly
5. a group of living things having similar characteristics
6. to take unfair advantage of
8. to pretend
10. to lessen in value; to belittle
12. hidden; undisclosed; not revealed
14. famed in story
16. to restate briefly
17. the nest of a bird of prey (alternative spelling)
18. a final demand
25. something worn as protection against evil
26. to make inferior by adding something
29. that cannot be maintained or defended
30. expression of sympathy
31. an article or item of food
33. a deadlock
34. fair; just
36. to do with the planning of military operations
37. a jeering remark; a taunt
38. bitterly and harshly severe
39. shriveled and shrunken
42. a side or face, as of a diamond
44. the highest point

13

Chapter Two

Word List 4

ABSTAIN	HISTRIONIC	PROXY
BIVOUAC	IMPROVIDENT	RECOURSE
CURTAIL	INHERENT	SCAPEGOAT
ENORMITY	INTROVERT	SUPPLANT
FISSURE	NEO-	TOME
GENERIC	PHILTRE	WHIMSICAL

Look up the words above in your dictionary. Note that many of them have more than one meaning. When you think that you know *all* the meanings of *all* the words, go on to the exercise below.

EXERCISE 4A

From the four choices following each phrase or sentence, you are to circle the letter preceding the one that is closest in meaning to the italicized word. Where the same word appears more than once, you should note that it is being used in different senses.

1. How many will *abstain*?
   (a) attend the meeting (b) remain behind (c) vote in the election (d) decline to vote

2. to *abstain* from drinking
   (a) become talkative (b) refrain (c) become drowsy (d) prevent others

3. to inspect the *bivouac*
   (a) line of defenses (b) parade of soldiers (c) equipment worn by a soldier (d) temporary military camp

4. to *curtail* costs
   (a) estimate roughly (b) reduce (c) figure out precisely (d) increase

5. the *enormity* of the offense
   (a) justification (b) outrageous nature (c) unexpected nature (d) unusual nature

6. a deep *fissure*
   (a) hole (b) groan (c) sigh (d) split

7. a *generic* term
   (a) old-fashioned (b) little-known (c) inclusive (d) accepted

8. a display of *histrionics*
   (a) military might (b) theatrical behavior (c) objects from the past (d) unbelievable rudeness

9. an *improvident* person
   (a) bold (b) wasteful (c) rude (d) cautious

10. *inherent* shyness
    (a) that rarely shows itself (b) that is a natural part of one (c) that one tries to cover up (d) that causes one great pain

11. an *introvert*
    (a) person who acts on impulse (b) person who is easily led (c) person who is stubborn and opinionated (d) person preoccupied with his or her own thoughts

12. *neo*-Gothic architecture
    (a) a new form of (b) the original form of (c) an early period of (d) a late period of

13. to drink the *philtre*
    (a) deadly poison (b) sleeping draught (c) bitter medicine (d) love potion

14. to appoint a *proxy*
    (a) committee that meets in secret (b) guardian of an orphaned child (c) a person authorized to act for another (d) lawyer who defends a penniless accused person

15. a last *recourse*
    (a) task that must be performed (b) source of help (c) chance given to a convicted criminal (d) statement by a dying person

16. a *scapegoat*
    (a) highly skilled mountain climber (b) object

of ridicule by others (c) person who takes the blame for others (d) person of low intelligence

17. to *supplant* someone
(a) beg a favor from (b) take the place of (c) have an evil influence on (d) hurt the feelings of

18. a large *tome*
(a) curved knife (b) bell (c) book (d) slab of rock

19. a *whimsical* fellow
(a) full of self-pity (b) bearded and moustached (c) red-faced and portly (d) full of odd notions

Check your answers against the correct ones given below. The answers are not in order; this is to prevent your eye from catching sight of the correct answers before you have had a chance to do the exercise on your own.

16c. 4b. 10b. 14c. 7c. 11d. 18c. 6d. 2b. 12a. 5b. 1d. 19d. 15b. 9b. 17b. 8b. 13d. 3d.

Look up in your dictionary all the words for which you gave incorrect answers. Only when you have done this should you go on to the next exercise.

EXERCISE 4B
Each word in Word List 4 is used several times in the following sentences to illustrate different meanings or usage. One of the sentences for each word uses the italicized word incorrectly. You are to circle the letter preceding the sentence.

1. (a) The doctor suggested that she *abstain* from starchy foods for a while. (b) He leads a very *abstemious* life, eating and drinking very little. (c) The requirements you refer to no longer *abstain*. (d) The final vote was 120-37 in favor, with 14 *abstentions*.

2. (a) If you don't *bivouac* my book, I'll report you. (b) The soldiers *bivouacked* along the east bank of the river. (c) A *bivouac* was set up for the night by the river bank.

3. (a) The heavy floods have severely *curtailed* traffic in the area. (b) The Magna Charta, signed in 1215, greatly *curtailed* the power of the king. (c) If you *curtail* two inches from the end, the length should be about right.

4. (a) I don't think she realizes the *enormity* of what she has done. (b) Hitler's *enormities* shocked the world. (c) Her leg has a slight *enormity* where she broke it.

5. (a) Molten rock *fissured* from the erupting volcano. (b) The *fissure* in the national party threatens to split it completely. (c) From a *fissure* in the rock came a thin trickle of water.

6. (a) She's a very *generic* person with a smile for everyone. (b) The word "ship" is a *generic* term for many kinds of large watercraft. (c) Drugs are often sold more cheaply under their *generic* names than under their trade names.

7. (a) We found her *histrionic* fits of temper rather tiresome. (b) The role of Hamlet is the favorite of most practitioners of the *histrionic* art. (c) We visited Grant's tomb and many other *histrionic* monuments.

8. (a) He is so *improvident* that his father makes him account for every penny he spends. (b) Her *improvidence* made her a burden on her friends in her old age. (c) She returned at a most *improvident* moment and caught them red-handed.

9. (a) She will *inherent* over five million dollars when her cousin dies. (b) We believe that certain rights are *inherent* and cannot be taken away. (c) These faults are *inherent* in the system, and we must just accept them.

10. (a) He is a very *introverted* person, difficult to draw into a discussion. (b) *Introverts* general-

15

ly do not make good salespeople. (c) It is an *introvertible* fact that Lincoln's main purpose was to save the Union.

11. (a) *Neo*-Nazis are active once again in some European cities. (b) The building had been redecorated completely and looked quite *neo*. (c) The years from 1760 to 1830 saw the flowering of *neo*-classical architecture.

12. (a) The charcoal is supposed to *philtre* impurities from the liquid. (b) He swallowed the *philtre* and fell in love immediately with the first person he saw. (c) The old woman sold *philtres* to the young people in the village.

13. (a) Anyone unable to attend the meeting may vote by *proxy*. (b) The two opposing groups try to *proxy* each other into giving way. (c) The chairperson decided that the *proxy* was not valid because it was unsigned. (d) A person unable to attend the meeting may appoint a *proxy* to vote for him or her.

14. (a) Many people have *recourse* to religion in time of trouble. (b) When she's in some difficulty, her older sister is always her first *recourse*. (c) She *recoursed* her uncle to let her have a few dollars.

15. (a) People usually look for a *scapegoat* when things go wrong. (b) The young man who joined the gang of thieves didn't suspect that they wanted him only as a *scapegoat*. (c) The old couple kept a few *scapegoats* tethered in the field behind their house.

16. (a) Someone had *supplanted* the young trees and scattered them about the park. (b) Leather has been *supplanted* by plastic in many everyday articles. (c) Mary Queen of Scots plotted to *supplant* Elizabeth I on the English throne.

17. (a) Two lines of poetry can sometimes tell us more than the weightiest *tome*. (b) Mr. Gradgrind had furnished his office with many large and imposing *tomes*. (c) The bells *tomed* mournfully for the great woman's funeral.

18. (a) Her uncle is a *whimsical* old fellow, full of entertaining ideas. (b) We don't take her *whimsical* notions too seriously. (c) The illustrations in the book have a *whimsical* quality that children love. (d) The gate swung *whimsically* on one loose hinge.

EXERCISE 4C

Prefixes
ab-, *abs-* (away from)
con- (with)
pro- (forward)
intro- (in, within)

Roots
tact, *tang* (touch)
duct, *duce* (lead)
ten, *tain* (hold)
vert (turn)

Suffixes
-ile (of, resembling)
-able, *-ible* (can be, may be)
-ure (act or process)

Using these Latin prefixes, roots, and suffixes (these terms are explained in the Introduction), construct words to fit the definitions below.

1. . . . . to bring forth; to bear; to yield

2. . . . . a holding, as of property, an office, or position

3. . . . . having to do with the sense of touch

4. . . . . to voluntarily do without

5. . . . . a person whose thoughts are turned inward

6. . . . . that can be held, defended, or maintained

7. .... to bring in, as a new feature

8. .... to lead away by force; to kidnap

9. .... a delicate feeling as to the right thing to say or do

10. .... that can be drawn or hammered thin without breaking (said of metals)

11. .... a touching or meeting

12. .... a tube or channel through which a gas or liquid moves

13. .... to change from one form or use to another

14. .... that can be touched or felt

15. .... to be a means for carrying; to transmit

WORDLY WISE 4

ENORMITY and *enormousness* are both based on the root word *norm* (Latin, *norma* — literally, "a carpenter's square"). Both words pertain to something "outside the measure" or "exceeding the rule." *Enormity*, however, has come to mean primarily an action hugely outside a moral norm or rule, hence greatly wicked. *Enormousness* (the state of being *enormous*) can equally well apply to virtuous things or acts (the *enormousness* of his generosity). It is always used when what is designated is physical immensity (the *enormousness* of the waves).

Distinguish between INTROVERT and *introspect*. An *introvert*, or *introverted* person, turns his or her thoughts inward, is self-absorbed. In contrast, the *extrovert* (Lesson 23) is a person who finds greatest interest in things outside himself or herself. An *introspective* person need not be an *introverted* one. To *introspect* is consciously to study one's own thoughts and feelings, to engage in self-examination or reflection.

Word List 5

APIARY	IMPEDIMENT	PSYCHE
CANT	INCOHERENT	REVELRY
DILETTANTE	INTERMEDIARY	SIBLING
ENVIRONS	IRE	TEDIUM
FROWZY	OBLIGATORY	TWIT
GRANARY	PRAGMATIC	

Look up the words above in your dictionary. Note that many of them have more than one meaning. When you think that you know *all* the meanings of *all* the words, go on to the exercise below.

EXERCISE 5A

From the four choices following each phrase or sentence, you are to circle the letter preceding the one that is closest in meaning to the italicized word. Where the same word appears more than once, you should note that it is being used in different senses.

1. a large *apiary*
   (a) place where birds are kept (b) place where bees are kept (c) place where apes are kept (d) place where reptiles are kept

2. thieves' *cant*
   (a) honor (b) stolen property (c) slang (d) methods of operation

3. pure *cant*
   (a) insincere talk (b) extreme delight (c) metal alloy (d) drivel

4. *canted* slightly
   (a) wobbling (b) moving (c) raised (d) tilted

5. a *dilettante*
   (a) person who cannot make up his or her mind (b) deceitful person (c) person who dabbles in the arts (d) expert in food and wines

6. the *environs* of the city
   (a) main thoroughfares (b) surrounding areas
   (c) parks and recreational areas (d) public
   buildings

7. *frowzy* clothes
   (a) tiny (b) secondhand (c) embroidered
   (d) slovenly

8. a large *granary*
   (a) field of wheat (b) building for storing
   grain (c) mill for grinding corn (d) loaf made
   of coarse grain

9. a minor *impediment*
   (a) obstacle (b) quarrel (c) accomplishment
   (d) official

10. an *incoherent* story
    (a) false (b) lengthy (c) confused (d) un-
    finished

11. a trusted *intermediary*
    (a) person not yet an adult (b) go-between
    (c) employee who supervises others (d) tem-
    porary remedy

12. a look of *ire*
    (a) anger (b) pity (c) sorrow (d) grief

13. *obligatory* contributions
    (a) optional (b) required (c) regular (d)
    charitable

14. a *pragmatic* approach
    (a) complicated (b) practical (c) simple
    (d) impractical

15. to probe the *psyche*
    (a) wound (b) mind (c) limits of space
    (d) depths of the sea

16. a night of *revelry*
    (a) deep thought (b) great unhappiness
    (c) deep remorse (d) merrymaking

17. *sibling* relationships
    (a) student-teacher (b) brother-sister

    (c) parent-child (d) church-state

18. to overcome the *tedium*
    (a) monotony (b) anxiety (c) pain (d) hand-
    icap

19. to *twit* someone
    (a) ignore (b) strike (c) tease (d) deceive

Check your answers against the correct ones
given below. The answers are not in order; this is to
prevent your eye from catching sight of the correct
answers before you have had a chance to do the
exercise on your own.

16d. 4d. 10c. 14b. 7d. 11b. 18a. 6b. 2c. 12a. 5c.
1b. 19c. 15b. 9a. 17b. 8b. 13b. 3a.

Look up in your dictionary all the words for
which you gave incorrect answers. Only when you
have done this should you go on to the next
exercise.

EXERCISE 5B
Each word in Word List 5 is used several times
in the sentences below to illustrate different
meanings or usage. One of the sentences for each
word uses the italicized word incorrectly. You are
to circle the letter preceding the sentence.

1. (a) Monkeys, chimpanzees, and other *apiary*
   creatures roamed the forest. (b) A sign outside the *apiary* said that honey was for sale.
   (c) He has been an *apiarist* for forty years and
   has over two hundred hives.

2. (a) I was sickened by the liar's *cant* about truth
   and honesty. (b) Thieves' *cant* is very hard for an
   outsider to understand. (c) The horses *canted*
   around the ring to the cheers of the crowd.
   (d) The roof was *canted* slightly.

3. (a) He has a *dilettante's* love of art but lacks
   the scholar's knowledge. (b) Much of the
   modern interest in art is little more than
   dilettantism. (c) Since they have a large fortune, they are free to *dilettante* at whatever
   they please.

4. (a) Over five hundred companies are located within the *environs* of the city. (b) More recreational facilities are needed for the city and its *environs*. (c) Oranges grow better in the warmer *environs* of the subtropics.

5. (a) The office of the two clerks consisted of a *frowzy* little room in the basement. (b) An old, *frowzily* dressed woman came to the door. (c) The table was covered with a piece of cheap *frowzy*.

6. (a) Egypt was the *granary* of the ancient world. (b) After such a wonderful harvest, the *granaries* were filled to bursting. (c) After they *granary* the corn, it is stored in large bins.

7. (a) Greek temples usually have a triangular *impediment* over the doorway. (b) One of the greatest *impediments* to travel was the poor condition of the roads. (c) He has a slight *impediment* in his speech that is noticeable only when he is excited.

8. (a) She looked *incoherently* at me as though scarcely able to believe her ears. (b) She was almost *incoherent* with rage. (c) The painter's ideas are expressed so *incoherently* in his later work that they are almost lost.

9. (a) She acts as an *intermediary* between the two groups. (b) He offered to *intermediary* the dispute, but no one had confidence in him. (c) The two countries were weary of the war and looked for an *intermediary* who would try to end it.

10. (a) That child would arouse the *ire* of a saint. (b) The people's *ire* is directed against the leaders who have misled them. (c) She began to *ire* in a loud voice when told she would have to wait.

11. (a) Attendance at the meeting is *obligatory* for all sophomores. (b) Obedience is *obligatory* for a soldier. (c) If you feel *obligatory* about it, I suggest you stay away from the meeting.

12. (a) She's very *pragmatic* and interested only in results. (b) He thinks Rosa takes a more *pragmatic* view of life's problems than does Michael. (c) We ignored her *pragmatics* and just carried on with what we had to do. (d) *Pragmatism* is a philosophy in which theories are tested by their practical application.

13. (a) Sigmund Freud probed deeply into the *psyche* of human beings. (b) Modern psychiatry is interested in the whole *psyche* and not just the conscious mind. (c) The person who committed this crime must be some kind of *psyche*.

14. (a) The old man would sometimes fall into a deep *revelry* in which he dreamed he was young again. (b) The sounds of *revelry* increased as the party continued into the night. (c) During Mardi Gras, the entire town is given over to *revelry*.

15. (a) He has four *siblings*: three sisters and a brother. (b) *Sibling* rivalry causes much family discord. (c) The man and woman regretted that their marriage had not been blessed with any *siblings*.

16. (a) A bedside radio helped to overcome the *tedium* of her stay in the hospital. (b) She preferred oil paints but had worked in other *tediums*. (c) The ceremony consists of nearly two hours of unrelieved *tedium*.

17. (a) The other men *twitted* him for always dressing so formally. (b) She did her best to ignore the *twits* of her friends. (c) A little bird began to *twit* with a high chirping sound.

EXERCISE 5C

From the four numbered choices, complete the following analogies by underlining the word that stands in the same relationship to the third word as the second word does to the first. An explanation of analogies is given in the Introduction.

1. aviary : apiary :: birds : (1) next (2) bees (3) zoo (4) apes

2. water : reservoir :: grain : (1) ripen (2) bread (3) reap (4) granary

3. indestructible:destroyed :: untenable:
(1) forgiven (2) held (3) released (4) used

4. miser:frugal :: wastrel: (1) improvident (2) incoherent (3) inopportune (4) rich

5. aerie:nest :: eagle: (1) bird (2) wing (3) beak (4) talon

6. salve:ointment :: opiate: (1) powder (2) drug (3) treatment (4) soothing

7. philter:filter :: rough: (1) smooth (2) coarse (3) boisterous (4) ruff

8. alto:tenor :: baritone: (1) bass (2) singer (3) base (4) deep

WORDLY WISE 5

ENVIRONS means "the districts around a city"; *environment* is a much broader term in general, meaning "the total of physical, social, and cultural factors influencing an individual or community."

INTERMEDIARY is a noun and means "a person acting as a go-between for two persons or parties." It can also be an adjective meaning "coming between two extremes," but *intermediate* is the more commonly used word for this meaning.

Etymology

Study the root and prefixes given below, together with the English words derived from them. Capitalized words are those given in the Word List. You should look up in a dictionary any words that are unfamiliar to you.

Prefixes: *inter-* (between) Latin — Examples: IN-TERMEDIARY, *inter*rupt *inter*mission
in- (not) Latin — Examples: IN-COHERENT, *in*sane, *in*decisive
co- (together) Latin — Examples: IN-COHERENT, *co*operate

Root: *here* (stick) Latin — Examples: INCO-HERENT, ad*here*

Word List 6

ASCETIC	IMPRECATIONS	PUNCTILIOUS
CRITERION	INDICT	SABOTAGE
DISCONCERT	INTRIGUE	SUBSTANTIAL
FACTION	LANCET	TESTIMONIAL
GARNER	PASTEURIZE	VALEDICTORY
HOMAGE	PRIMORDIAL	

Look up the words above in your dictionary. Note that many of them have more than one meaning. When you think that you know *all* the meanings of *all* the words, go on to the exercise below.

EXERCISE 6A

From the four choices following each phrase or sentence, you are to circle the letter preceding the one that is closest in meaning to the italicized word. Where the same word appears more than once, you should note that it is being used in different senses.

1. an *ascetic* life
(a) given over to pleasure (b) brief but happy (c) of rigorous self-denial (d) long and illustrious

2. the chief *criterion*
(a) member of a governing body (b) standard used in judging (c) ingredient (d) judge in a law court

3. to *disconcert* someone
(a) angrily accuse (b) suddenly confuse (c) fiercely defend (d) deliberately ignore

4. a large *faction*
(a) part of an area of land (b) group working against other groups (c) share of whatever is produced (d) number that cannot be divided

5. bitter *faction*
(a) hatred (b) quarreling (c) grief (d) medicine

6. to *garner* wealth
(a) scorn (b) gather in (c) give away (d) hunger for

7. to pay *homage*
   (a) money demanded by robbers (b) payment for damages (c) respect and honor (d) false compliments

8. to utter *imprecations*
   (a) protests (b) curses (c) warnings (d) complaints

9. to *indict* a person
   (a) charge with a crime (b) suspect of a crime (c) convict of a crime (d) find not guilty of a crime

10. one who *intrigues* me
    (a) interests (b) baffles (c) ignores (d) despises

11. to *intrigue* against the queen
    (a) speak out (b) wage open war (c) bear a grudge (d) plot

12. a person's *intrigues*
    (a) secret thoughts (b) secret love affairs (c) fits of temper (d) attempts to appear mysterious

13. The *lancet* went deep.
    (a) arrowhead (b) bullet wound (c) cutting remark (d) surgeon's knife

14. to *pasteurize* milk
    (a) extract water from (b) spread the cream throughout (c) destroy bacteria in (d) add water to

15. *primordial* people
    (a) Renaissance (b) earliest (c) modern (d) medieval

16. a *punctilious* account
    (a) fictitious (b) constantly interrupted (c) exact (d) glibly delivered

17. acts of *sabotage*
    (a) criminal neglect (b) deliberate destruction (c) unthinking cruelty (d) worship

18. a *substantial* house
    (a) partly finished (b) solid (c) cheaply made (d) identical

19. a *substantial* amount
    (a) large (b) fair (c) partial (d) small

20. a *substantial* businessperson
    (a) wealthy (b) overweight (c) uneducated (d) self-made

21. to receive many *testimonials*
    (a) requests for favors (b) offers of help (c) tokens of esteem (d) helpful suggestions

22. to listen to the *valedictory*
    (a) message of greeting (b) farewell address (c) triumphant flourish of trumpets (d) mournful piece of music

Check your answers against the correct ones given below. The answers are not in order; this is to prevent your eye from catching sight of the correct answers before you have had a chance to do the exercise on your own.

9a. 14c. 10a. 19a. 18b. 6b. 3b. 17b. 4b. 1c. 21c. 22b. 20a. 5b. 8b. 12b. 16c. 11d. 7c. 15b. 2b. 13d.

Look up in your dictionary all the words for which you gave incorrect answers. Only when you have done this should you go on to the next exercise.

EXERCISE 6B
Each word in Word List 6 is used several times in the following sentences to illustrate different meanings or usage. One of the sentences for each word uses the italicized word incorrectly. You are to circle the letter preceding the sentence.

1. (a) *Ascetic* acid is the chief ingredient of vinegar. (b) She led an *ascetic* life in which worldly pleasure had no part. (c) He is no *ascetic*; he loves good food, good wine, good company. (d) *Ascetisicm* is practiced as a way of life by these monks.

2. (a) What was the *criterion* used in selecting the winners? (b) No exact *criterion* exists to make forecasting completely accurate. (c) Certain *criteria* are being established as we learn more about the problem. (d) There is one *criteria* that must always be taken into account.

3. (a) A terrible *disconcert* of noise came from the band as it warmed up. (b) The lawyer was obviously *disconcerted* by the surprise witness. (c) She has a *disconcerting* habit of asking the most intimate questions. (d) Don't allow the sudden change of plans to *disconcert* you.

4. (a) *Factional* disputes have prevented the party from moving ahead. (b) The party broke up into numerous *factions*, each accusing the others of betraying the cause. (c) The park is divided into four *factions*, one for each season of the year. (d) Bitter *faction* broke out on the Senate floor when the bill was debated.

5. (a) The *garners* are filled to overflowing with golden grain. (b) These art treasures have been *garnered* from the four corners of the earth. (c) When the harvest has been *garnered*, then the farmers may rest. (d) I *garner* that the president does not intend to seek reelection this year.

6. (a) Lincoln's Gettysburg Address paid *homage* to the men who had died in battle. (b) "May I speak to your *homage*?" said the servant to her mistress. (c) *Homage* to a feudal lord was required in return for the protection he gave those under him. (d) They bowed their heads in *homage* to their leader.

7. (a) He hurled *imprecations* at those who had defied him. (b) Do you understand fully all the *imprecations* of the offer? (c) They feared to rebel openly and contented themselves with muttered *imprecations*.

8. (a) He sat down to *indict* a letter to his brother in Africa. (b) She was *indicted* before a grand jury and sent for trial. (c) The president *indicted* those Americans who remain indifferent to the problems facing the nation.

9. (a) "Here is an *intriguing* mystery," said the detective. (b) Rasputin was a master of *intrigue* at the Court of Czar Nicholas II. (c) The money was *intrigued* from her by a gang of clever rogues. (d) Benjamin Franklin describes several youthful *intrigues* in his autobiography.

10. (a) The army consisted of four thousand foot soldiers and a thousand *lancets*. (b) The doctor opened the boil on the patient's neck with a single stroke of her *lancet*. (c) A *lancet* is usually pointed and has two sharp cutting edges.

11. (a) Milk is *pasteurized* by being heated at 145°F for thirty minutes. (b) The doctor *pasteurized* the wound by pouring iodine on it.

12. (a) It is very *primordial* of you to eat with your fingers. (b) We know a great deal about those *primordial* ancestors of ours, the Neanderthal people. (c) It is claimed that the sun and the planets were created out of a *primordial* mass of gas.

13. (a) He is a *punctilious* host, attentive to the smallest detail. (b) She arrived *punctiliously* at the time agreed upon. (c) A *punctilious* record is kept of the production of each worker.

14. (a) *Sabotage* is suspected in yesterday's explosion on the battleship Defiant. (b) Police arrested four *saboteurs* who were attempting to blow up the bridge. (c) Someone tried to *sabotage* the meeting by switching off the public address system. (d) Pieces of *sabotage* from the wrecked ship were seen floating on the surface.

15. (a) Can you *substantial* your statement that you were at home that night? (b) We are in

substantial agreement as to what needs to be done. (c) She received a *substantial* share of the estate on her uncle's death. (d) You get a *substantial* meal and a comfortable bed for ten dollars.

16. (a) The design of the building is a *testimonial* to the architect who planned it. (b) A *testimonial* dinner will be given for the retiring senator. (c) Before giving a *testimonial* in court, a witness must take an oath. (d) She was presented with the key to the city as a *testimonial* to her years of service.

17. (a) The student having the highest marks will be class *valedictorian* at the graduation exercises. (b) In her *valedictory* address she referred to the lasting friendships made in school. (c) To speak beyond the allotted time is perfectly *valedictory*. (d) The general, in a short *valedictory*, thanked his soldiers for their support.

EXERCISE 6C

This exercise is divided into two parts: Part A deals with synonyms, Part B with antonyms (these terms are explained in the Introduction). Allow only fifteen minutes for this test. If you cannot answer a question, go on to the next one without delay. If you have time left over at the end, go back and try to fill in unanswered questions.

26 or over correct:	excellent
21 to 25 correct:	good
20 or under correct:	thorough review of A exercises indicated

Part A (Synonyms)

Underline the word that is most *similar in meaning* to the CAPITALIZED word or phrase.

1. STANDARD
moral acme criterion strategic facsimile

2. PLOT
paean enormity cant **intrigue** impediment

3. PRAISE
gibe homage depreciate disconcert indict

4. GATHER IN
articulate abstain garner recapitulate **exploit**

5. CURSE
imprecation aerie apiary fissure **gibe**

6. FAREWELL ADDRESS
paean valedictory acme proxy **homage**

7. SLANG
bivouac apiary tome cant dogmatic

8. TEASE
articulate garner indict ire twit

9. SLOVENLY
primordial incoherent frowzy **inopportune** slapstick

10. ANGER
ire cant fissure psyche scathing

11. PRACTICAL
elective sibling criterion **pragmatic** loquacious

12. SPLIT
sabotage fissure disconcert twit philtre

13. INCLUSIVE
substantial whimsical obligatory intermediary generic

14. LOVE POTION
lancet testimonial philtre paean stipend

15. BOOK
tome opiate cant alto amulet

Part B (Antonyms)

Underline the word that is most nearly *opposite in meaning* to the CAPITALIZED word or phrase.

16. ENHANCE
disconcert depreciate intrigue eradicate partake

17. ABUNDANCE
enormity intermediary statutory paucity improvident

18. SCORN
supplant eradicate lionize ameliorate articulate

19. COMPULSORY
paucity stalemate curtail elective punctilious

20. EXCITABLE
incoherent inopportune gesticulate impediment imperturbable

21. SUITABLE
inopportune frowzy sabotage legendary scapegoat

22. SILENT
comestible strategic loquacious moral generic

23. OBEDIENT
fractious elective vainglorious equitable punctilious

24. INDULGE
abstain abdicate adulterate scuttle introvert

25. INCREASE
abstain sabotage intrigue curtail garner

26. THRIFTY
frowzy improvident primordial loquacious inopportune

27. OPTIONAL
inherent whimsical elective enormity obligatory

28. GLOOM
introvert psyche revelry apiary cant

29. SLIGHT
criterion frowzy wizened fractious substantial

30. CARELESS
punctilious whimsical histrionic incoherent inherent

WORDLY WISE 6

ASCETIC (pronounced ə-SET-ik) means "practicing rigorous self-denial." *Acetic* (pronounced ə-SEET-ik) means "of or relating to the acid in vinegar." (Vinegar is composed mainly of *acetic* acid.)

The plural of CRITERION is *criteria*, but *criterions* is also correct.

Under feudal law, the recipient of a fief became the vassal or "man" of his lord by performing a ritual act—usually by kneeling and placing his hands in those of the lord. In highly feudalized France the ceremony was known as *hommage* (from *homme*, "man"). HOMAGE, derived from the French, is sometimes pronounced with a silent *h*. To pay or do *homage* today is simply to honor, regard with reverence, or pay tribute to someone.

INDICT and *indite* are homonyms and both are pronounced in-DYT. *Indict* means "to charge with some offense," while *indite* means "to set down in writing."

Etymology

Study the roots given below, together with the English words derived from them. Capitalized words are those given in the Word List. You should look up in a dictionary any words that are unfamiliar to you.

Roots: *prim* (first) Latin – Examples: *PRIMORDIAL*, *primi*tive, *prim*ary

test (witness) Latin – Examples: *TESTIMONIAL*, *test*ify, *test*ament

ACROSS

1. a love potion
7. an insufficient number or amount (1)
10. a temporary military camp
11. curses
12. a regular fixed sum, as a salary (1)
15. deliberate destruction of property
16. anything done to show honor or respect
18. noisy merrymaking
19. the authority to act for someone else
20. one who dabbles in any of the arts
22. a standard by which judgments may be made
25. a pointed, two-edged surgeon's knife
28. a person whose thoughts are directed inward
29. to gather in and store
30. a book, especially a large book
32. to make fun of; to tease
34. a farewell speech
37. solid; strong
38. acting as a go-between
40. one who bears the blame for others
43. something done to show respect or thanks
46. to voluntarily do without
47. anything that obstructs or hinders
48. the districts around a city
49. required; legally or morally binding
50. rigorously self-denying
51. testing the validity of by results
52. the mind in its entirety; the soul

DOWN

1. to do with earliest times; primitive
2. lacking foresight; lacking thrift
3. a turning for help or protection
4. full of odd notions or fancies
5. to momentarily confuse cr upset
6. too positive in stating opinions (2)
7. to destroy bacteria in milk by heating
8. anger
9. a place where bees are kept
13. being a natural part of something or someone
14. a combining form meaning "a new form of"
17. a building for storing grain
21. not clearly connected; disjointed; rambling
23. to cut short; to reduce
24. dirty and untidy; slovenly
26. the condition of being tiresome and wearisome
27. insincere speech
31. a group that dissents within a larger group
33. attentive to every detail
35. to take the place of by force or scheming
36. having to do with actors or acting
38. to plot secretly or underhandedly
39. great wickedness
40. a brother or sister
41. inclusive of a whole kind or class
42. a split or crack
44. to charge with a crime
45. the second highest part of four-part harmony (3)

Chapter Three

Word List 7

AMBIDEXTROUS	IDIOM	MINION
BLATANT	IMPIOUS	PROCLIVITY
CREMATE	INFIDELITY	REBUT
DISCURSIVE	INTERPOLATE	SINECURE
EXPOUND	LITERATE	TARIFF
GRUELING		

Look up the words above in your dictionary. Note that many of them have more than one meaning. When you think that you know *all* the meanings of *all* the words, go on to the exercise below.

EXERCISE 7A

From the four choices following each phrase or sentence, you are to circle the letter preceding the one that is closest in meaning to the italicized word. Where the same word appears more than once, you should note that it is being used in different senses.

1. an *ambidextrous* person
   (a) expert in more than one profession (b) having a strong desire to succeed (c) uncertain as to which of two courses to follow (d) able to use both hands with equal ease

2. a *blatant* lie
   (a) skillfully concealed (b) offensively obvious (c) hastily thought up (d) subtly confusing

3. to *cremate* the body
   (a) view formally (b) examine for signs of disease (c) prepare for burial (d) burn to ashes

4. a *discursive* speech
   (a) fascinating (b) pointed (c) rambling (d) terse

5. to *expound* a theme
   (a) criticize strongly (b) generally agree with (c) state in detail (d) demonstrate the falsity of

6. a *grueling* task
   (a) extremely distasteful (b) severely demanding (c) seemingly unending (d) surprisingly easy

7. to understand an *idiom*
   (a) statement with a double meaning (b) phrase not meant literally (c) signal previously agreed upon (d) remark in a foreign language

8. the *idiom* of the Elizabethans
   (a) literature taken as a whole (b) manners and customs (c) ideas (d) style of speaking

9. an *impious* remark
   (a) foolish (b) lacking reverence (c) cruelly deceptive (d) solemn

10. a person's *infidelity*
    (a) refusal to take part (b) lack of understanding (c) lack of faithfulness (d) religious beliefs

11. to *interpolate* comments
    (a) discover the meaning of (b) mutter under one's breath (c) insert (d) leave unsaid

12. a *literate* person
    (a) involved (b) educated (c) important (d) excitable

13. How many are *literate*?
    (a) capable of learning (b) receiving higher education (c) unable to read or write (d) able to read and write

14. a *minion* of the king
    (a) secret enemy (b) royal boat (c) faithful follower (d) son who will succeed to the throne

15. a strong *proclivity*

(a) hatred (b) inclination (c) purpose (d) denial

16. to *rebut* a statement
    (a) support with evidence (b) oppose by argument (c) issue (d) agree with

17. looking for a *sinecure*
    (a) completely trustworthy person (b) wise teacher (c) easy, well-paying job (d) forgiveness of a sin

18. a high *tariff*
    (a) lookout tower (b) tax on imports (c) wall around a piece of property (d) tax on land

19. the inn's *tariff*
    (a) bill of fare (b) guest register (c) rating as to quality (d) scale of charges

Check your answers against the correct ones given below. The answers are not in order; this is to prevent your eye from catching sight of the correct answers before you have had a chance to do the exercise on your own.

3d. 13d. 8d. 17c. 9b. 15b. 19d. 1d. 5c. 16b. 4c. 10c. 14c. 7b. 11c. 18b. 6b. 2b. 12b.

Look up in your dictionary all the words for which you gave incorrect answers. Only when you have done this should you go on to the next exercise.

EXERCISE 7B

Each word in Word List 7 is used several times in the following sentences to illustrate different meanings or usage. One of the sentences for each word uses the italicized word incorrectly. You are to circle the letter preceding the sentence.

1. (a) He took a somewhat *ambidextrous* view of the proposal. (b) *Ambidextrous* tennis players are rare. (c) Her skill as a surgeon was aided by her *ambidexterity*.

2. (a) Her *blatant* refusal to admit her guilt was quite in character. (b) Radio commercials are sometimes so *blatant* that they turn people away from the product advertised. (c) The level of noise continues to rise, with motorcyclists the most *blatant* offenders. (d) It was quite *blatant* to everyone that the defendant was guilty.

3. (a) The body was *cremated*, and the ashes scattered to the wind. (b) The number of people favoring *cremation* over burial is increasing. (c) The fire brigade arrived too late to prevent the house from being completely *cremated*.

4. (a) In the course of her long and *discursive* speech she touched on many points of interest. (b) The roads through the mountain are narrow and *discursive*, often impassable in winter. (c) This is a big, sprawling book, perhaps too *discursive* for the general reader.

5. (a) The personality of the teacher is as important as the subject she *expounds*. (b) He was *expounded* from the navy for conduct unbecoming an officer. (c) Baseball players will *expound* on their favorite games for hours at a time. (d) She *expounded* in a very clear manner the difference between the two groups.

6. (a) He threw himself at the feet of the queen, *grueling* for mercy. (b) The engine is subjected to the most *grueling* laboratory tests. (c) The marathon is a *grueling* footrace run over 26 miles and 385 yards or approximately 42 kilometers.

7. (a) "To catch someone's eye" is an *idiom* meaning "to be noticed by someone." (b) It was *idiomatic* of him to allow the children to accompany them. (c) Many of our most familiar sayings are *idiomatic* and cannot be taken literally. (d) Country people speak a quite different *idiom* from city folk.

8. (a) The slightest change in the church service would be considered *impious* by the congregation. (b) She *impiously* tried to sneak into the cinema without paying. (c) He thought that a

27

deathbed repentance could make up for an *impious* life. (d) The girl's *impious* remarks shocked her father, who is a devout man.

9. (a) They complained often of each other's *infidelity* but to no avail. (b) They claim to be faithful, but their deeds proclaim their *infidelity*. (c) Her *infidelity* to hold a position of trust soon became obvious.

10. (a) No one was able to *interpolate* exactly what the sign meant. (b) Much additional material has been *interpolated* into the text. (c) "If I may *interpolate* a remark," she began diffidently. (d) The professor had *interpolated* a number of revisions into the thesis.

11. (a) The book is a *literate* attempt to bridge the gap between art and science. (b) The people in the remoter parts of the country are *literately* starving. (c) Forty years ago only ten percent of the population was *literate*. (d) They like to gather together their more *literate* friends for an evening's discussion.

12. (a) The director sent one of her *minions* to find out the reason for the delay. (b) Cut off from their people and surrounded by *minions*, the rulers led a life of neglectful ease. (c) He had once held a *minion* post of some kind in the king's service. (d) Police officers are sometimes called "*minions* of the law."

13. (a) We dismounted and made our way down the *proclivity* on foot. (b) His *proclivity* for gossiping is well known in the village. (c) She has a touching *proclivity* for championing lost causes.

14. (a) The wall had recently been *rebutted* with stout timbers. (b) His claim was quickly *rebutted* by the judge. (c) It was easy to *rebut* her opponent's statement.

15. (a) Many jobs in the city government were little more than *sinecures*. (b) He was a *sinecure*, able to discuss intelligently the merits of different wines. (c) A job in the Peace Corps, with its long hours and low pay, is no *sinecure*.

16. (a) We climbed to the top of the *tariff* and looked down at the people far below. (b) A *tariff* of two cents a pound was imposed. (c) *Tariffs* are imposed on imported goods to protect home industries. (d) The hotel is comfortable, and the *tariff* is quite reasonable.

EXERCISE 7C

In each of the sentences below a word is omitted. From the four words provided, select the one that best completes the sentence. Allow ten minutes for this test. If you cannot answer a question, go on to the next one without delay. If you have time left over at the end, go back and try to fill in unanswered questions.

18 or over correct:	excellent
14 to 17 correct:	good
13 or under correct:	thorough review of A exercises indicated

1. The reviewer's comments had been .... into the text.
   indicted interpolated ameliorated supplanted

2. Discussions reached a(n) ....
   and were broken off.
   criterion impediment stalemate bivouac

3. He is a wicked man, and all his talk about brotherly love is pure ....
   facsimile minion sinecure cant

4. The children grew .... because they were tired and hungry.
   discursive fractious punctilious pragmatic

5. We widened the .... in the rock by driving in a wedge.
   fissure facet proclivity faction

6. His .... for making uninformed decisions often got him into trouble.
   paean proclivity enormity impediment

7. Someone has been trying to . . . .
. . . . our efforts by spreading
false stories.
sabotage exploit adulterate relegate

8. The country was presented with a(n)
. . . . that it could not ignore.
proxy ultimatum tariff valedictory

9. Attendance at school assemblies is . . . .
punctilious strategic obligatory comestible

10. He found it very hard to live on such a small
. . . .
acme stipend tariff granary

11. For the benefit of latecomers I will
. . . . what has been said so far.
rebut expound recapitulate interpolate

12. The Indianapolis 500 is a . . . .
test of driver and machine.
vainglorious grueling scathing loquacious

13. The queen was forced to . . . .
and was succeeded by her daughter.
abdicate interpolate abstain supplant

14. Is there any evidence of . . . .
between the two groups?
paucity collusion proclivity condolence

15. I suggest that you . . . . from
intense exercise for at least a month.
expound depreciate abdicate abstain

16. She acted as a(n) . . . . between
the two rival groups.
criterion intermediary turnkey valedictory

17. In his novels he tries to . . . . the
needs and wishes of his characters.
recourse disconcert articulate abstain

18. She hurled . . . . at her disloyal
followers.
slapstick imprecations exploits testimonials

19. My visits to the country are greatly . . . .
. . . . now that I have no car.
curtailed supplanted disconcerted abstained

20. The . . . . life of a monk was not
for him because he enjoyed his pleasures too
much.
ulterior untenable elective ascetic

WORDLY WISE 7

Both PROCLIVITY and *propensity* refer to
a natural inclination or leaning. *Proclivity*, however, expresses especially an inherent inclination
toward something objectionable. (He had a
proclivity for violence.)

SINECURE is pronounced *SINE - ə - cure*
or *SIN - ə - cure*.

Etymology

Study the roots and prefixes given below,
together with the English words derived from
them. Capitalized words are those given in the
Word List. You should look up in a dictionary any
words that are unfamiliar to you.

Prefixes: *ambi* (both) Latin — Examples: *AMBI-*
DEXTROUS, *ambi*guous
im- (not) Latin — Examples: *IM*PIOUS,
*im*possible, *im*practical
(Review) *in-* (not) Latin — Example:
*IN*FIDELITY
Roots: *dext* (right-hand) Latin — Examples:
AMBI*DEXT*ROUS, *dext*erity, *dext*rous
fid (trust) Latin — Examples: IN*FI-*
DELITY, con*fide*

Word List 8

AMBIVALENCE	IMPERATIVE	PROGENITOR
CHOLER	INCAPACITATE	RESILIENT
CURFEW	INNOVATION	STAMINA
DISMANTLE	INVETERATE	TEMPERATE
FATHOM	MAGNITUDE	WAYWARD
HEMP	OCTAGON	

Look up the words above in your dictionary.
Note that many of them have more than one meaning. When you think that you know *all* the meanings
of *all* the words, go on to the following exercise.

EXERCISE 8A

From the four choices following each phrase or sentence, you are to circle the letter preceding the one that is closest in meaning to the italicized word. Where the same word appears more than once, you should note that it is being used in different senses.

1. a mood of *ambivalence*
   (a) black despair (b) indifference to the feelings of others (c) simultaneous conflicting feelings (d) carefree gaiety

2. filled with *choler*
   (a) joy (b) pity (c) sadness (d) anger

3. to ignore the *curfew*
   (a) warning shot fired over a ship (b) order not to visit certain places (c) signal of impending danger (d) time to be off the streets

4. to *dismantle* machinery
   (a) unload (b) take apart (c) erect (d) damage

5. to *dismantle* a ship
   (a) ready for sea duty (b) remove the fittings from (c) attack and disable (d) raise from the sea bottom

6. five *fathoms*
   (a) units of weight (b) units of depth (c) units of area (d) units of volume

7. to *fathom* the meaning
   (a) forget (b) remember (c) understand thoroughly (d) suggest indirectly

8. strong *hemp*
   (a) white clay used in pottery (b) plant fibers used in rope (c) willow branches used in baskets (d) drink made from coconuts

9. It is *imperative*.
   (a) absolutely necessary (b) utterly useless (c) long delayed (d) unthinkable

10. the *imperative* mood

(a) used for commands (b) used for questions (c) used for statements (d) used for requests

11. to *incapacitate* someone
    (a) inconvenience (b) make use of (c) disable (d) entertain

12. to resist the *innovation*
    (a) corroding effect of dampness (b) introduction of something new (c) invasion by a foreign army (d) effects of old age

13. an *inveterate* gambler
    (a) losing (b) habitual (c) confident (d) lucky

14. the *magnitude* of it
    (a) greatness (b) purpose (c) cause (d) lack

15. to draw an *octagon*
    (a) four-sided figure (b) five-sided figure (c) eight-sided figure (d) nine-sided figure

16. My *progenitors* lived here.
    (a) children (b) ancestors (c) followers (d) descendants

17. the *progenitor* of the airplane
    (a) driving unit (b) forerunner (c) design (d) passenger load

18. *resilient* grass
    (a) lush (b) springy (c) parched (d) damp

19. a *resilient* personality
    (a) highly excitable (b) easily depressed (c) child-like (d) able to recover quickly

20. great *stamina*
    (a) resistance to wear (b) internal pressure (c) natural ability (d) staying power

21. a *temperate* zone
    (a) subject to great changes in temperature (b) neither very hot nor very cold (c) on or near the poles (d) on or near the equator

22. a *temperate* reply

(a) spiteful (b) moderate (c) excited (d) angry

23. a *wayward* child
(a) independent (b) willful (c) loving (d) beautiful

24. the *wayward* wind
(a) gentle (b) strong (c) changeable (d) constant

Check your answers against the correct ones given below. The answers are not in order; this is to prevent your eye from catching sight of the correct answers before you have had a chance to do the exercise on your own.

6b. 13b. 11c. 18b. 7c. 17b. 1c. 23b. 15c. 22b. 10a. 14a. 9a. 21b. 4b. 2d. 24c. 12b. 19d. 5b. 16b. 3d. 20d. 8b.

Look up in your dictionary all the words for which you gave incorrect answers. Only when you have done this should you go on to the next exercise.

EXERCISE 8B

Each word in Word List 8 is used several times in the sentences below to illustrate different meanings or usage. One of the sentences for each word uses the italicized word incorrectly. You are to circle the letter preceding the sentence.

1. (a) His feelings toward her are marked by *ambivalence*; he both loves and hates her. (b) Her country's foreign policy caused her to have *ambivalent* feelings toward the land of her birth. (c) The *ambivalence* of the question confused him, because he didn't know which way to take it.

2. (a) *Choler*, a once deadly disease that was widespread in Europe, has been largely eliminated. (b) In a terrible fit of *choler*, the queen imprisoned her eldest son. (c) He's a red-faced, *choleric* gentleman, given to violent outbursts.

3. (a) There is a ten o'clock *curfew* for all people under eighteen. (b) The *curfew* rings at nine o'clock as a signal for everyone to be off the streets. (c) He looked at the *curfew* and saw that it was past the time when he should be at home. (d) The governor will not lift the *curfew* until order has been restored in the town.

4. (a) We were somewhat *dismantled* to see the train leaving the station just as we arrived. (b) The ship was *dismantled* before being broken up for scrap. (c) The engine was *dismantled*, cleaned, and put back together. (d) Price controls were *dismantled* immediately after the war.

5. (a) We tried to *fathom* the mystery of her disappearance. (b) The ship was lost in two hundred *fathoms* of water. (c) No one knew the *fathom* to the mystery. (d) The *fathom*, now fixed at six feet, was the distance from fingertip to fingertip of a man's outstretched arms.

6. (a) Before the advent of nylon, ropes were made almost exclusively of *hemp*. (b) The boxes were *hemped* together with strong ropes. (c) *Hemp* is a tall Asiatic plant of the mulberry family.

7. (a) The command "Run!" is expressed in the *imperative* mood. (b) The *imperative* city of Rome was the center of a great empire. (c) It is *imperative* that I see the manager without delay. (d) In an *imperative* tone she told the driver to stop.

8. (a) They *incapacitated* the wine into quart bottles. (b) She was *incapacitated* by a broken leg. (c) The illness had *incapacitated* him and rendered him unfit for active work.

9. (a) The club has made a number of *innovations* since last year. (b) The speaker was given a tremendous *innovation* by the crowd. (c) Electric lighting was a startling *innovation* in the 1890s.

10. (a) It was their *inveterate* habit to take a small glass of brandy before retiring. (b) The man is known to be an *inveterate* liar. (c) She is such an *inveterate* person that her own father threw her out.

11. (a) The *magnitude* of the area was about four square miles. (b) The publishing of this book is an event of the first *magnitude*. (c) The country had not expected to wage a war of this *magnitude*. (d) The *magnitude* of her discovery is only now being appreciated.

12. (a) A regular *octagon* has eight 135° angles. (b) *Octagonal* houses were once fashionable in this part of the state. (c) The two houses are *octagonally* opposite each other.

13. (a) The best all-around student is made class *progenitor*. (b) The mystery tales of Edgar Allan Poe are the *progenitors* of the modern detective story. (c) Our *progenitors* built this land and passed it on to us as a trust.

14. (a) We *resiliented* the attack with ease. (b) Natural rubber is more *resilient* than the synthetic kind. (c) She is a *resilient* person who is never down for long.

15. (a) She trains every day to increase her *stamina*. (b) He begins to *stamina* when he gets excited. (c) Great *stamina* is needed to compete in the marathon.

16. (a) The speaker was *temperate* in her approach to the problem. (b) I was obliged to ask her to *temperate* her language. (c) This plant flourishes best in a *temperate* climate. (d) He warned against even the *temperate* use of alcohol.

17. (a) The boat, tossed hither and yon by *wayward* winds, at last reached port. (b) There was a small island about five miles to *wayward* of the ship. (c) She had spent a year in a school for *wayward* children. (d) The story deals with two young people in the grip of a *wayward* passion.

EXERCISE 8C

In each pair of sentences or phrases below, the italicized word is used once literally and once metaphorically (explanations of these terms are given in the Introduction). Write (L) where the word is used literally; write (M) where the word is used metaphorically.

1. *Sift* the flour. ( ) The detective must *sift* the evidence. ( )

2. I could a tale *unfold*. ( ) Help me to *unfold* the blanket. ( )

3. She is a *fountain* of wisdom. ( ) We drank water from the *fountain*. ( )

4. a *cloudy* sky ( ) His future looks *cloudy*. ( )

5. a rich, *meaty* broth ( ) a *meaty* role for an actor ( )

6. a *wooden* stare ( ) a *wooden* spoon ( )

7. an *oily* manner ( ) an *oily* surface ( )

8. an *avalanche* of mail ( ) an *avalanche* in the mountains ( )

9. a *watered-down* wine ( ) a *watered-down* speech ( )

10. a tree-shaded *avenue* ( ) to explore every *avenue* in the case ( )

WORDLY WISE 8

The four medieval humors (or bodily fluids) were *choler* (bile), *melancholer* (black bile), *phlegm* (mucus), and *sang* (blood). It was believed that if these were all in perfect balance, a person would be "in good humor." In the event of an imbalance, a person could be *choleric* (angry), *melancholy* (sad), *phlegmatic* (sluggish), or *sanguine* (cheerful). These terms have survived in the language even though modern physiology is no longer based on the four humors. Thus, CHOLER still means "anger."

Classical myths personified destiny as three women who spun and finally cut off a person's "thread" of life. STAMINA ("threads") became a Latin metaphor for "life," and in English means "vigor" or "capacity to resist fatigue or disease."

Etymology

Many common words are based on Greek or Latin numbers. The word OCTAGON, for example, comes from the Greek word *octa* (eight). Greek number prefixes with words based on them, include the following:

mono (one) Examples: *mon*arch, *mono*tony
bi (two) Examples: *bi*ped, *bi*cycle
tri (three) Examples: *tri*angle, *tri*plets
tetra (four) Examples: *tetra*rch, *tetra*hedron
penta (five) Examples: *penta*gon, *penta*thlon
hexa (six) Examples: *hexa*gon, *hexa*meter
hepta (seven) Examples: *hepta*gon, *hepta*meter
octa (eight) Examples: *octo*pus, *octa*gon
ennea (nine) Example: *ennea*d (nine gods)
deca (ten) Examples: *deca*de, *deca*gon
hecto (hundred) Example: *hecto*meter
kilo (thousand) Examples: *kilo*gram, *kilo*watt

Word List 9

AUTOPSY	IMPERIAL	OVERWROUGHT
COMPUNCTION	INFATUATED	QUANDARY
DEBUT	INSTILL	RETICENT
EXPOSITORY	IRRATIONAL	STERILIZE
GLUTINOUS	MARAUDER	UNWITTING
HOMILY		

Look up the words above in your dictionary. Note that many of them have more than one meaning. When you think that you know *all* the meanings of *all* the words, go on to the following exercise.

EXERCISE 9A

From the four choices following each phrase or sentence, you are to circle the letter preceding the one that is closest in meaning to the italicized word. Where the same word appears more than once, you should note that it is being used in different senses.

1. to conduct an *autopsy*
   (a) inquiry into some aspect of government (b) investigation into criminal activities (c) examination to determine the cause of death (d) search for religious truth

2. to lack *compunction*
   (a) strength (b) remorse (c) health (d) forethought

3. to make one's *debut*
   (a) first appearance (b) final appearance (c) apologies (d) farewells

4. *expository* material
   (a) hidden (b) usable (c) explanatory (d) uncovered

5. a *glutinous* mixture
   (a) sticky (b) watery (c) explosive (d) strong smelling

6. We listened to the *homily*.
   (a) farewell address (b) piano recital (c) lecture on a moral theme (d) speech of welcome

7. *imperial* rule
   (a) cruel and tyrannical (b) by the people (c) by an emperor (d) by elected representatives

8. to wear an *imperial*
   (a) gold crown (b) small, pointed beard (c) scarlet robe (d) plumed hat

9. an *imperial* manner
   (a) majestic (b) calm (c) sullen (d) excitable

10. *infatuated* with her
    (a) bored (b) angry (c) foolishly in love (d) disgusted

11. to *instill* honesty
    (a) revere (b) impart (c) scorn (d) pretend

12. to *instill* oil
    (a) purify (b) convert (c) reuse (d) introduce drop by drop

13. an *irrational* act

(a) showing lack of concern for others (b) illegal (c) done to irritate or annoy (d) not governed by reason

14. Is that the *marauder*?

(a) leader (b) attacker (c) beggar (d) designer

15. to be *overwrought*

(a) hard to understand (b) suffering from nervous strain (c) unbelievably beautiful (d) past the retirement age

16. an *overwrought* design

(a) graceful (b) too elaborate (c) too crude (d) too geometrical

17. in a *quandary*

(a) state of perplexity (b) place where stone is dug out (c) area of soft, marshy ground (d) heavy, horse-drawn wagon

18. a *reticent* person

(a) of below average intelligence (b) disinclined to speak (c) extremely nervous (d) showing great courage

19. to *sterilize* the wound

(a) apply a dressing to (b) insert stitches in (c) make free from germs (d) probe carefully

20. to *sterilize* an animal

(a) painlessly put to death (b) follow the tracks of (c) make incapable of reproduction (d) steal and pass off as one's own

21. an *unwitting* accomplice

(a) unaware (b) uncooperative (c) unwilling (d) eager

22. an *unwitting* insult

(a) not malicious (b) not openly stated (c) not intended (d) calculated

Check your answers against the correct ones given in the next column. The answers are not in order; this is to prevent your eye from catching sight of the correct answers before you have had a chance to do the exercise on your own.

8b. 2b. 18b. 6c. 21a. 11b. 14b. 20c. 12d. 19c. 7c. 9a. 1c. 22c. 15b. 5a. 13d. 16b. 3a. 10c. 17a. 4c.

Look up in your dictionary all the words for which you gave incorrect answers. Only when you have done this should you go on to the next exercise.

EXERCISE 9B

Each word in Word List 9 is used several times in the sentences below to illustrate different meanings or usage. One of the sentences for each word uses the italicized word incorrectly. You are to circle the letter preceding the sentence.

1. (a) The *autopsy* showed that the man had died of cancer of the lung. (b) Under this medical plan you get a free *autopsy* from your doctor every year. (c) The doctor should order an *autopsy* if she is unsure of the cause of death.

2. (a) Route 17 runs in *compunction* with Highway 4 for about six miles. (b) They steal from rich and poor without *compunction*. (c) She had no *compunction* about taking her friend's money.

3. (a) His *debut* as an actor took place when he was only five years old. (b) Her parents plan a grand ball for her *debut* into society. (c) After rehearsing for weeks, the school band will *debut* at tonight's concert. (d) Each girl makes a *debut* to her escort, who bows in return.

4. (a) The large trunk in the basement was the *expository* for all our junk. (b) The students in this class need practice in *expository* writing.

5. (a) Mix the flour and water together until they have a *glutinous* consistency. (b) His *glutinous* habits are hard to conceal since he weighs nearly 300 pounds. (c) The meal con-

sisted of a stale piece of bread and a bowl of *glutinous* stew.

6. (a) She delivered a *homily* to the teenagers on the perils of strong drink. (b) He's a *homily* boy but very good-natured.

7. (a) In A.D. 410 the *imperial* city of Rome was sacked by the invading Goths. (b) The empress was careful to do nothing that would *imperial* her throne. (c) The loss of India in 1947 marked the end of British *imperial* rule. (d) He thought that if he grew an *imperial*, he would look more distinguished.

8. (a) She is *infatuated* with the idea of sailing around the world. (b) Her *infatuation* for the boy ended as suddenly as it had begun. (c) The young boy thought he was in love with the singer when he was merely *infatuated* with her. (d) Early in the morning the ground is *infatuated* with dew.

9. (a) He *instilled* a love of reading into his children. (b) The university plans to *instill* its new chancellor next week. (c) A little of this solution is *instilled* into the eyes of newborn babies.

10. (a) A person in love often acts *irrationally*. (b) A few items of food were rationed, but most kinds were *irrational*. (c) They must have been extremely angry to do such an *irrational* thing as set fire to the money.

11. (a) The sounding of the alarm frightened away the *marauder*. (b) We heard the coach *marauder* the team for not trying harder. (c) The isolated village was under frequent attack by bands of *marauding* soldiers.

12. (a) The doctor suggested that her *overwrought* patient take up a hobby. (b) His forced and *overwrought* style spoils what could have been an interesting book. (c) If you *overwrought* the boy too hard, his work will suffer.

13. (a) I am in a *quandary* as to which of the

offers to accept. (b) The professor asked us a *quandary* to which no one knew the answer.

14. (a) Few radio disc jockeys could truthfully be described as *reticent*. (b) The ship made its way slowly and *reticently* through the great ice packs. (c) The more we questioned him, the greater was his *reticence*. (d) Though *reticent* about her past life, she had much to say about everything else.

15. (a) She was *sterilized* with terror at the screams that came from the darkness. (b) Heavy doses of radiation can *sterilize* workers who lack adequate protection. (c) The dentist's instruments are *sterilized* before use.

16. (a) She managed to keep the party a secret from her *unwitting* friends. (b) She is willing to overlook any *unwitting* mistakes on your part. (c) Humans are born the most helpless and *unwitting* of animals. (d) They were *unwitting* us at our own game.

EXERCISE 9C

This exercise is divided into two parts: Part A deals with synonyms, Part B with antonyms (these terms are explained in the Introduction). Allow only fifteen minutes for this test. If you cannot answer a question, go on to the next one without delay. If you have time left over at the end, go back and try to fill in unanswered questions.

26 or over correct:	excellent
22 to 25 correct:	good
21 or under correct:	thorough review of A exercises indicated

Part A (Synonyms)

Underline the word that is most *similar in meaning* to the CAPITALIZED word or phrase.

1. INCLINATION
   infidelity expository criterion proclivity faction

2. STAYING POWER
testimonial sinecure stamina quandary tedium

3. UNFAITHFULNESS
proclivity impediment revelry fissure infidelity

4. REMORSE
quandary ambivalence recourse compunction enormity

5. INSERT
literate relegate incapacitate temperate interpolate

6. ANGER
homily stamina choler autopsy ambivalence

7. STICKY
wayward glutinous overwrought reticent resilient

8. DISABLE
dismantle sterilize instill incapacitate interpolate

9. EXPLANATORY
proclivity quandary punctilious substantial expository

10. UNDERSTAND
fathom expound interpolate indict abstain

11. URGENT
glutinous unwitting overwrought imperative imperial

12. ATTACKER
marauder minion sinecure faction sibling

13. SPRINGY
temperate wayward resilient ambidextrous discursive

14. MODERATE
impious temperate tedium criterion punctilious

15. SEVERELY DEMANDING
expository glutinous reticent grueling blatant

Part B (Antonyms)
Underline the word that is most nearly *opposite in meaning* to the CAPITALIZED word or phrase.

16. ERECT
incapacitate fathom dismantle rebut interpolate

17. PROMOTE
instill rebut debut expound relegate

18. AWARE
inveterate unwitting literate irrational impious

19. DISCREET
reticent imperative discursive blatant imperial

20. OCCASIONAL
wayward discursive inveterate substantial resilient

21. STEADFAST
grueling blatant wayward inveterate resilient

22. REVERENT
overwrought infatuated incoherent impious fractious

23. INFECT
sterilize rebut instill twit supplant

24. RELAXED
discursive blatant literate inveterate overwrought

25. TERSE
punctilious discursive unwitting resilient temperate

26. TALKATIVE
reticent expository dilettante obligatory discursive

27. SCATTER

garner expound dismantle instill pasteurize

28. NEAT

temperate imperial wayward blatant frowzy

29. REASONABLE

ambidextrous punctilious discursive irrational substantial

30. EXTOL

expound debut instill sterilize depreciate

WORDLY WISE 9

DEBUT was brought into English from the French, and its pronunciation (either *DAY-byoo* or *day-BYOO*) reflects this.

IMPERIAL means "of or pertaining to an empire or emperor." (Britain was once a great *imperial* power.) *Imperious* is derived from the same Latin word *imperare* ("to command") but has come to mean "domineering; overbearing." (His *imperious* manner offended those who had to work with him.)

INSTILL can also be spelled with one *l* — *instil*.

Wrought was the past participle of the Old English verb *wyrcan* ("to work"). In the 15th century the modern *worked* replaced the earlier form and *wrought* is now archaic except in senses denoting fashioning, shaping or decorating, especially by hand (a well-*wrought* bowl; *wrought* iron). OVERWROUGHT thus means "overworked" (an *overwrought* teacher) or "overdone; overdecorated" (an *overwrought* silver pattern).

ACROSS

1. lacking in reverence for God
3. a time by which people must be off the streets
5. indicating authority or command
9. a natural tendency in human nature
12. a tax on imported goods
15. a plant fiber used in rope-making
16. a new method, custom, or device
17. one that roams about and attacks
19. unpredictable; erratic
20. able to read and write
21. deliberately loud or obtrusive
22. that serves to explain
24. springing back into shape or position
25. a follower, especially a servile follower
26. greatness of size or extent
29. a state of puzzlement or perplexity
32. an eight-sided figure
34. able to use either hand with equal ease
37. to argue or prove that a statement is wrong
40. firmly fixed or established; habitual
42. wandering from topic to topic; rambling
45. great anger; wrath
46. to relinquish voluntarily, as a throne (3)
47. to make free from germs
48. not done on purpose; not intended
49. to introduce into over a period of time (alternative spelling)
50. to burn to ashes, as a dead body
51. to insert into (writing or conversation)

DOWN

1. of an empire, emperor, or empress
2. an ancestor in a direct line
4. a unit of depth equal to 6 feet
5. inspired with an unreasoning passion
6. an examination to determine the cause of death
7. a characteristic way of speaking or writing
8. to state in detail
10. to disable
11. disloyalty to one's promise or faith
13. too nervous or excited; strained
14. that does not make sense; not logical
18. having a sticky, glue-like consistency
23. very talkative (2)
27. a large book (4)
28. a first appearance before the public
30. simultaneous conflicting emotions
31. a feeling of regret for something done
33. severely demanding
35. disinclined to speak
36. to take apart
38. neither too hot nor too cold (said of climate)
39. an undemanding, well-paying job
41. a daring deed (1)
43. resistance to fatigue, hardship, or illness
44. a long talk on a moral and uplifting subject

Chapter Four

Word List 10

ADDLED	FILIAL	ORNITHOLOGIST
CAUTERIZE	GAMESTER	PHILISTINE
CONGESTION	HARANGUE	RATIONALIZE
DISINTERESTED	INDIGNITY	SALUTARY
EXHALE	MAUSOLEUM	TACITURN

Look up the words above in your dictionary. Note that many of them have more than one meaning. When you think that you know *all* the meanings of *all* the words, go on to the exercise below.

EXERCISE 10A

From the four choices following each phrase or sentence, you are to circle the letter preceding the one that is closest in meaning to the italicized word. Where the same word appears more than once, you should note that it is being used in different senses.

1. an *addled* mind
   (a) independent (b) confused (c) sharp (d) calm

2. an *addled* egg
   (a) raw (b) scrambled (c) rotten (d) speckled

3. to *cauterize* a wound
   (a) apply disinfectant to (b) stitch up (c) burn with a hot iron (d) bind up

4. *congestion* in the streets
   (a) panic (b) overcrowding (c) misery (d) joy

5. *congestion* of the lungs
   (a) deterioration of the cells (b) overaccumulation of matter (c) complete failure to function (d) insufficient supply of blood

6. a *disinterested* observer
   (a) bored (b) impartial (c) discontented (d) unaware

7. to *exhale* slowly
   (a) grow tired (b) breathe out (c) die (d) breathe in

8. to *exhale* a gas
   (a) condense (b) compress (c) give off (d) change the form of

9. *filial* love
   (a) of parents for their child (b) of a child for its parents (c) of a citizen for his or her country (d) of a wife and husband for each other

10. a professional *gamester*
    (a) gambler (b) hunter (c) sportswoman (d) game warden

11. a violent *harangue*
    (a) long, scolding speech (b) fit of coughing (c) quarrel (d) attack with sticks or clubs

12. to accept the *indignity*
    (a) high office (b) insulting treatment (c) symbol of office (d) high honor

13. a family *mausoleum*
    (a) monumental tomb (b) annual reunion (c) ancestral home (d) coat of arms

14. an enthusiastic *ornithologist*
    (a) expert on the oceans (b) expert on birds (c) expert on warfare (d) expert on bullfighting

15. a *philistine*
    (a) uncultured and narrow-minded person (b) criminal who acts as an informer (c) person of wide-ranging interests (d) person who lives far beyond his or her means.

16. Don't *rationalize* what you did.
    (a) seek reasons to justify (b) offer any apologies for (c) try to understand (d) attempt to cover up

17. a *salutary* effect
    (a) slight (b) startling (c) beneficial (d) damaging

18. a *taciturn* person
    (a) ill-mannered (b) deceitful (c) habitually silent (d) steadfastly loyal

Check your answers against the correct ones given below. The answers are not in order; this is to prevent your eye from catching sight of the correct answers before you have had a chance to do the exercise on your own.

8c. 12b. 18c. 16a. 3c. 2c. 7b. 13a. 10a. 14b. 1b. 5b. 17c. 6c. 11a. 9b. 15a. 4b.

Look up in your dictionary all the words for which you gave incorrect answers. Only when you have done this should you go on to the next exercise.

EXERCISE 10B

Each word in Word List 10 is used several times in the sentences below to illustrate different meanings or usage. One of the sentences for each word uses the italicized word incorrectly. You are to circle the letter preceding the sentence.

1. (a) He *addled* the eggs with a wooden spoon and poured them into the pan. (b) Her speeches are designed to appeal only to the *addled* minds of her supporters. (c) Of the six eggs we bought, four were *addled*.

2. Warts can be removed by being *cauterized* with a red-hot needle. (b) If the wound is left untended, it will begin to *cauterize*. (c) In the past, wounds were *cauterized* with hot irons to prevent infection from setting in.

3. (a) She *congestioned* that the bad weather was the cause of the high food prices. (b) The system of one-way streets is designed to reduce traffic *congestion*. (c) Doctors are attempting to reduce the *congestion* in the patient's lungs. (d) Nasal *congestion* is one symptom of a cold.

4. (a) He sought the *disinterested* advice of a trusted friend. (b) Her *disinterested* kindness to us will never be forgotten. (c) The first requirement for a trial by law is a *disinterested* judge. (d) Their parents offered them a trip to Europe, but they were completely *disinterested* in the idea.

5. (a) The marshes *exhale* a peculiar-smelling gas. (b) The engine *exhaled* a loud gurgling sound and then stopped. (c) Take a deep breath; then *exhale* slowly. (d) *Exhaled* air has more carbon dioxide than air breathed in.

6. (a) The son grew more and more *filial* toward his parents and eventually left home. (b) Many children disregard their *filial* obligations. (c) He thinks that *filial* obedience is the first requirement for a happy home.

7. (a) A crowd of *gamesters* stood around the roulette table. (b) You should never *gamester* more than you can afford to lose.

8. (a) The father *harangued* his children for being late. (b) She embarked on an emotional *harangue* that was directed against just about everyone. (c) If the speech seems too *harangue*, we can always tone it down a little.

9. (a) She was secretly furious at the *indignities* that were heaped upon her. (b) With great *indignity* he walked out of the room. (c) She was forced to suffer one *indignity* after another.

10. (a) *Mausoleum* was poured over the body before it was wrapped for burial. (b) The body was laid to rest in the *mausoleum* that had been built for it. (c) The house was as gloomy as a *mausoleum*.

11. (a) *Ornithologists* are meeting today to discuss the migration patterns of Canada geese. (b) J.J. Audubon was a famous American *ornithologist* whose pictures of birds are known all over the world. (c) She has written

on the nesting habits of birds and other *ornithologist* subjects.

12. (a) The townspeople were accused of being *philistines* because their town had no theaters or art galleries. (b) She spoke of the strained relations that always exist between the artist and *philistine* society. (c) *Philistines* are tearing down our historic buildings and putting up concrete and glass office blocks in their places. (d) The new developments have *philistined* the historic town.

13. (a) Don't try to *rationalize* your misdeeds by blaming your friends. (b) We *rationalized* our defeat by blaming the weather. (c) We urged her to stop *rationalizing* and admit her selfishness. (d) Since water was so short, the survivors in the lifeboat decided to *rationalize* the supply.

14. (a) After a week at the health spa, she was her old *salutary* self again. (b) Swimming and other *salutary* pastimes are encouraged at the camp. (c) Showing photographs of auto accidents has a *salutary* effect on careless drivers.

15. (a) "Silent Cal" Coolidge was one of our more *taciturn* presidents. (b) The two women had a *taciturn* agreement not to interfere with each other's affairs. (c) The *taciturnity* of New Englanders is proverbial.

EXERCISE 10C

From the four numbered choices, complete the analogies below by underlining the word that stands in the same relationship to the third word as the second word does to the first. An explanation of analogies is given in the Introduction.

1. triangle:octagon :: three: (1) five (2) six (3) seven (4) eight

2. mile:distance :: fathom: (1) feet (2) height (3) ocean (4) depth

3. rational:reason :: literate: (1) read (2) learn (3) fault (4) feel

4. paternal:father :: filial: (1) child (2) mother (3) brother (4) friend

5. criteria:criterion ::species: (1) specie (2) plant (3) animal (4) species

6. silent:talkative :: taciturn: (1) reticent (2) loquacious (3) glutinous (4) resilient

7. question:command :: interrogative: (1) order (2) imperative (3) genitive (4) ask

8. ameliorate:improve :: incapacitate: (1) discover (2) disable (3) discontinue (4) disturb

WORDLY WISE 10

DISINTERESTED means "lacking motives of self-interest"; *uninterested* means "lacking interest." (A judge should be *disinterested* in a case; he or she should not be *uninterested* in it.) These two words are quite different in meaning. They are sometimes erroneously thought of as interchangeable.

A FILIAL relationship is that between child and parent; *filial* describes the status, behavior, or feelings of the child, especially in the sense of what is becoming or appropriate to the relationship. (Harry was never noted for *filial* obedience.) *Paternal* and *maternal* refer to the relationship between parent and child; *fraternal* to that between brothers; *sororal* to that between sisters.

Distinguish between SALUTARY and *salutatory*, meaning "expressing salutations or welcome." (The speaker began with *salutatory* remarks to the guests at the meeting.)

Word List 11

ANARCHY	FORTE	PALLIATIVE
CENSER	GRAPHIC	PRODIGIOUS
DEFILE	HERESY	REDOUBTABLE
ENTOURAGE	INSIDIOUS	SINUOUS
EXPUNGE	MEDIATE	THRALL

Look up the words above in your dictionary. Note that many of them have more than one meaning. When you think that you know *all* the meanings of *all* the words, go on to the following exercise.

From the four choices following each phrase or sentence, you are to circle the letter preceding the one that is closest in meaning to the italicized word. Where the same word appears more than once, you should note that it is being used in different senses.

1. a state of *anarchy*
   (a) rule by a dictator (b) social and political unrest (c) deliberately imposed terror (d) complete political disorder

2. A *censer* is needed.
   (a) official examiner of books, plays, etc. (b) canopy to protect against sun and rain (c) guard rail to hold people back (d) vessel for burning incense

3. through the *defile*
   (a) cleansing fire (b) pool of dirty water (c) narrow tube (d) narrow pass

4. to be *defiled*
   (a) dishonorably discharged (b) made unclean (c) lined up (d) completely ignored

5. a large *entourage*
   (a) group of companies (b) group of attendants (c) group of performers (d) group of tourists

6. to *expunge* the entry
   (a) mark (b) remove (c) question (d) consider

7. This is his *forte*.
   (a) great weakness (b) particular skill (c) immediate purpose (d) immediate need

8. Play it *forte*.
   (a) loudly (b) softly (c) slowly (d) quickly

9. a *graphic* description
   (a) wordy (b) vivid (c) vague (d) written

10. the *graphic* arts
    (a) verbal (b) industrial (c) pictorial (d) ancient

11. accused of *heresy*
    (a) giving false evidence in a court of law (b) holding views contrary to those officially taught (c) burning one's own property to collect insurance (d) plotting to overthrow a legally elected government

12. an *insidious* scheme
    (a) treacherous (b) unworkable (c) effective (d) costly

13. to *mediate* a dispute
    (a) work for a settlement of (b) be the cause of (c) aggravate (d) attempt to prolong

14. *palliative* remedies
    (a) that are adopted as a last resort (b) that ease without curing (c) that are worse than the disease (d) that are effective but slow working

15. a *prodigious* amount
    (a) varying (b) enormous (c) unknown (d) small

16. a *redoubtable* foe
    (a) long-standing (b) formidable (c) treacherous (d) timorous

17. a *sinuous* line
    (a) thin (b) strong (c) winding (d) dotted

18. in *thrall*
    (a) peace (b) danger (c) bondage (d) trust

19. to be a *thrall*
    (a) farmer (b) worker (c) soldier (d) slave

Check your answers against the correct ones given below. The answers are not in order; this is to prevent your eye from catching sight of the correct answers before you have had a chance to do the exercise on your own.

3d. 10c. 17c. 4b. 15b. 5b. 14b. 16b. 19d. 7b. 9b. 1d. 11b. 13a. 12a. 8a. 2d. 18c. 6b.

Look up in your dictionary all the words for which you gave incorrect answers. Only when you have done this should you go on to the next exercise.

EXERCISE 11B

Each word in Word List 11 is used several times in the sentences below to illustrate different meanings or usage. One of the sentences for each word uses the italicized word incorrectly. You are to circle the letter preceding the sentence.

1. (a) The people objected to the *anarchy* who was sent to rule over them. (b) *Anarchy* reigned in the land during those first days of the revolution. (c) He referred to those *anarchic* days when the city was ruled by armed mobs roaming the streets.

2. (a) The heavy smell of burning incense rose from the *censer*. (b) The *censer* refused to approve the play unless certain changes were made.

3. (a) They that touch pitch will be *defiled*. (b) The rabbi was convinced that those people who had broken into the temple had *defiled* the house of God. (c) We made our way with difficulty through the *defile*. (d) The *defile* of the water supply is caused by the discharge of industrial wastes into it.

4. (a) Jane completed her *entourage* of the buildings and left to write up her report. (b) Movie stars never go anywhere unless they are surrounded by their *entourages*. (c) The prince and princess and their *entourage* occupied five floors of the hotel during their visit.

5. (a) Not a word has been *expunged* from this book. (b) He *expunged* on the subject with great enthusiasm. (c) He could not *expunge* from his heart the great bitterness he felt. (d) The school *expunged* the episode from his record.

6. (a) The next passage is played *forte*. (b) In a very *forte* voice he demanded admittance.

(c) Acting is her *forte*.

7. (a) She is a *graphic* writer and therefore always interesting to read. (b) He moved *graphically* through the building, checking for fire hazards. (c) The book describes *graphically* what it is like to be under fire. (d) The *graphic* arts include drawing, painting, and engraving.

8. (a) She became *heretical* when she saw that no one believed her story. (b) *Heretics* were burned at the stake in the Middle Ages. (c) Martin Luther was tried for *heresy* when he defied the Church of Rome. (d) Many scientific views regarded as *heretical* a few years ago are now generally accepted.

9. (a) The disease, unnoticed by the patient, works *insidiously* to destroy the cells of the body. (b) By spreading rumors and committing other *insidious* acts, the plotters hoped to weaken the government. (c) The heavy rains have made the path by the river very *insidious*.

10. (a) She was able to *mediate* a settlement very quickly. (b) It is better for management and labor to *mediate* their differences than to engage in strikes or lockouts. (c) The *mediate* cause of the fire is not known.

11. (a) All work and no play makes for a very *palliative* life. (b) The situation is so serious that *palliative* measures are no longer adequate. (c) A doctor will sometimes prescribe a *palliative* for a disease she cannot cure.

12. (a) They looked *prodigiously* at him when he said he had magical powers. (b) This country is *prodigiously* wealthy. (c) That girl has a *prodigious* appetite. (d) He was able to perform *prodigious* feats of strength.

13. (a) The merchant found himself face to face with the *redoubtable* pirate Captain Morgan. (b) Their great wealth and family background make them *redoubtable* opponents in the election. (c) She is *redoubtably* qualified for the position she seeks.

43

14. (a) The *sinuous* movements of a cat are strikingly graceful. (b) The river lay below them, a *sinuous* silver ribbon. (c) She had the *sinuous* strength of a trained athlete.

15. (a) The Viking marauders killed some of the villagers and made *thralls* of others. (b) Her great wit held them in *thrall*. (c) The pirate chief threatened to *thrall* the people of the village. (d) They spoke of exchanging the *thralldom* of earth for the joys of heaven.

EXERCISE 11C

oligos (few)	*patros* (father)
hieros (sacred)	*matri* (mother)
a or *an* (without)	*mono* (one)

Combine a prefix or root derived from one of the Greek words above with the Greek root derived from *archos* ("ruler") and construct words to match the definitions below.

1. .... a system of government by a single hereditary ruler

2. .... a system of tribal rule with a man as leader

3. .... a state of complete political disorder and lawlessness

4. .... a system of tribal rule with a woman as leader

5. .... a group of persons arranged in order of rank or grade

6. .... government in which only a few persons have ruling power

The Greek root *arch (os)* may also mean "chief," "first," or "ancient." Give definitions for the words below, which use this root in one of these meanings.

7. *arch*eozoic ....

8. *arch*etype ....

9. *arch*itect ....

10. *arch*ives ....

11. *arch*angel ....

12. *arch*aic ....

WORDLY WISE 11

A CENSER is a vessel for holding incense; a *censor* (see Word List 25) is an official who has power to examine letters or works written or produced to ensure that they contain nothing considered dangerous or unacceptable to the established authorities.

A mountain pass so narrow that a group of people can pass through it only in single file is called a DEFILE. The word comes from the French verb *défiler* which means "to march in single file."

FORTE is pronounced *FOR-ti* or *FOR-tay* when it is a musical term meaning "loud." It is pronounced *FORT* when it means a particular skill or something one does particularly well.

Word List 12

AQUEOUS	GREGARIOUS	QUADRUPLE
CHASTE	INCLEMENT	REPLETE
DEMORALIZE	MALADROIT	SPECTRAL
EUTHANASIA	MENDICANT	TRANSITION
EXTENUATING	PANORAMA	TRIUMVIRATE
GALA		

Look up the words above in your dictionary. Note that many of them have more than one meaning. When you think that you know *all* the meanings of *all* the words, go on to the following exercises.

EXERCISE 12A

From the four choices following each phrase or sentence, you are to circle the letter preceding the one that is closest in meaning to the italicized word. Where the same word appears more than once, you should note that it is being used in different senses.

1. *aqueous* deposits
   (a) made by wind (b) made by water (c) made by volcanic eruption (d) made by decayed vegetable matter

2. a *chaste* person
   (a) naturally shy (b) morally pure (c) highly intelligent (d) totally unpredictable

3. a *chaste* design
   (a) expensively executed (b) heavily ornate (c) severely plain (d) highly unusual

4. to *demoralize* them
   (a) put new heart into (b) reduce the number of (c) weaken the spirit of (d) reduce the strength of

5. to favor *euthanasia*
   (a) the abolition of all laws (b) killing as an act of mercy (c) selective breeding to improve the race (d) the belief that all religions are essentially the same

6. *extenuating* factors
   (a) that tend to unite (b) that make something seem less serious (c) that make something seem more complicated (d) that tend to divide

7. a *gala* occasion
   (a) festive (b) mournful (c) memorable (d) formal

8. a *gregarious* person
   (a) enjoying solitude (b) enjoying the company of others (c) disinclined to speak (d) talkative

9. *inclement* weather
   (a) sunny (b) stormy (c) changeable (d) unvarying

10. an *inclement* act
    (a) thoughtful (b) unkind (c) unlawful (d) just

11. *maladroit* handling
    (a) clumsy (b) skillful (c) delicate (d) using one hand only

12. surrounded by *mendicants*
    (a) flatterers (b) beggars (c) insects (d) enemies

13. to admire the *panorama*
    (a) display of pictures (b) parade of animals (c) staged reenactment of an historical event (d) comprehensive view

14. to *quadruple* something
    (a) call into question (b) strongly emphasize (c) reduce to one fourth (d) increase fourfold

15. *replete* with learned references
    (a) satisfied (b) filled (c) bored (d) concerned

16. a *spectral* figure
    (a) substantial (b) ghostly (c) commanding (d) slight

17. a period of *transition*
    (a) change (b) uncertainty (c) stability (d) unrest

18. to set up a *triumvirate*
    (a) ruling body of three (b) welcome for a returning hero (c) law that must be renewed every three years (d) defensive barrier

Check your answers against the correct ones given below. The answers are not in order; this is to prevent your eye from catching sight of the correct answers before you have had a chance to do the exercise on your own.

8b. 12b. 16b. 3c. 2b. 7a. 13d. 10b. 14d. 18a. 1b. 5b. 17a. 6b. 11a. 9b. 15b. 4c.

Look up in your dictionary all the words for which you gave incorrect answers. Only when you have done this should you go on to the next exercise.

EXERCISE 12B

Each word in Word List 12 is used several times in the sentences below to illustrate different meanings or usage. One of the sentences for each word uses the italicized word incorrectly. You are to circle the letter preceding the sentence.

1. (a) The material is suspended in an *aqueous* solution. (b) *Aqueous* rocks are those laid down by the action of water. (c) They gave us a bowl of *aqueous* soup and a piece of bread.

2. (a) A design had been *chaste* around the edge of the silver dish. (b) He led a *chaste* and ordered life with his uncles. (c) Leaving the *chaste* and silent hallway, we entered the warm living room.

3. (a) She loved to *demoralize* on what was wrong with the country. (b) The defeat totally *demoralized* the army. (c) The purpose of bombing the city was to *demoralize* the inhabitants. (d) Poor leadership has a *demoralizing* effect on those led.

4. (a) A feeling of deep *euthanasia* came over Karen, and she fell into a deep sleep. (b) Although doctors are dedicated to saving lives, some favor *euthanasia* in certain cases. (c) *Euthanasia,* a means of ending the suffering of incurably sick people, is discussed in this article.

5. (a) She seemed to be *extenuating* that I was somehow at fault. (b) The boy's extreme youth is an *extenuating* factor in the case. (c) There were no *extenuating* circumstances that might have led the judge to impose a lighter sentence.

6. (a) The *gala* will end with a display of fireworks. (b) Everyone was dressed in *gala* costumes for the occasion. (c) The marriage of the shy electrician and the gracious bank teller was a *gala* occasion. (d) Every April the villagers *gala* the arrival of spring with dances on the green.

7. (a) Penguins are *gregarious* creatures and live together in flocks numbering in the thousands. (b) They make a somewhat *gregarious* living by selling firewood from door to door. (c) They are *gregarious* people, never happier than when with a crowd of friends.

8. (a) The base salary is twenty thousand dollars with yearly *inclements* of one thousand dollars. (b) The show will be held indoors if the weather is *inclement.* (c) One expects harsh sentences from such an *inclement* judge.

9. (a) Linda *maladroited* herself out of the situation with great skill. (b) The situation was handled very *maladroitly*, and everyone's feelings were hurt. (c) It is possible for a person to be a great diplomat and a *maladroit* politician.

10. (a) *Mendicant* friars, who lived on the gifts of those they met, were a common sight in the Middle Ages. (b) She always carried a few coins to give to any *mendicants* she met on her travels. (c) These herbs have *mendicant* properties useful in the treatment of certain diseases.

11. (a) A broad-brimmed *panorama* shielded his face from the sun. (b) Niagara Falls offers an unforgettable *panorama* to the awe-struck tourist. (c) This book presents with great vividness the whole *panorama* of American history.

12. (a) The population has *quadrupled* in the past forty years. (b) Forty is the *quadruple* of ten. (c) A *quadruple* amputee is one who has lost both arms and both legs. (d) It is a newsworthy event when a mother gives birth to *quadruples* and all four live.

13. (a) Our water supply will be *repleted* unless there is rain soon. (b) The book is *replete* with apt quotations. (c) The Indianapolis 500 is a race *replete* with thrills and spills.

14. (a) They shuddered when the Headless Horse-

man pointed a *spectral* finger at them. (b) At the sight of the *spectral* the two men screamed and beat a hasty retreat. (c) The *spectral* shapes that frightened us so much were probably made by marsh gas being exhaled from the bog.

15. (a) He had intended to buy the house but changed his mind before the *transition* could be completed. (b) The *transition* from childhood to adulthood is not an easy one. (c) Architecture is currently undergoing a *transition* to a freer use of space. (d) *Transitional* passages have been inserted to bridge the different scenes.

16. (a) Following Caesar's assassination, Rome was ruled by a *triumvirate*. (b) This world-famous *triumvirate* of painters merits the respect of all art lovers. (c) Her *triumvirate* march ended with her being crowned empress.

EXERCISE 12C

This exercise combines synonyms and antonyms. You are to underline the word which is *either* most similar in meaning *or* most nearly opposite in meaning to the CAPITALIZED word. Underline only one word for each question after deciding that it is *either* an antonym *or* a synonym and write A (for antonym) or S (for synonym) after the capitalized word. Allow only ten minutes for this test. If you cannot answer a question, go on to the next one without delay. If you have time left over at the end, go back and try to fill in unanswered questions.

18 or over correct: excellent
14 to 17 correct: good
13 or under correct: thorough review of A
                        exercises indicated

1. HARMFUL .....
chaste palliative spectral inclement salutary

2. IMPARTIAL .....
extenuating forte taciturn insidious disinterested

3. HEARTEN .....
demoralize cauterize censer rationalize redoubtable

4. GHOSTLY .....
mausoleum spectral filial aqueous inclement

5. WINDING .....
philistine addled extenuating sinuous irrational

6. MITIGATING .....
salutary pragmatic extenuating insidious irrational

7. TALKATIVE .....
addled harangue disinterested filial taciturn

8. BEGGAR .....
marauder thrall censer mendicant progenitor

9. POLLUTE .....
exhale mediate defile demoralize incapacitate

10. MERCIFUL .....
inclement disinterested chaste extenuating palliative

11. INSCRIBE .....
mediate expunge harangue exhale fathom

12. IMPURE .....
aqueous spectral chaste forte temperate

13. CONFUSED .....
graphic sinuous prodigious replete addled

14. FESTIVE .....
chaste maladroit inclement gala wayward

15. SKILLFUL .....
disinterested maladroit resilient philistine taciturn

16. FILLED .....
congestion replete aqueous magnitude proclivity

17. SOLITARY . . . . .

taciturn gregarious maladroit impious discursive

18. CHANGE . . . . .

anarchy idiom heresy transition rebut

19. ORDER . . . . .

anarchy congestion heresy idiom criterion

20. VISTA . . . . .

mendicant gala panorama minion environs

WORDLY WISE 12

AQUEOUS, "of, relating to, or having the characteristics of water," occurs in scientific terminology especially, and is used narrowly. Often it describes a substance chemically (*aqueous* ammonia, *aqueous* meteor). *Watery* may refer to substances that resemble water in texture, thin fluidity, paleness, or lack of taste (*watery* paste, *watery* blues and greens, *watery* soup).

Etymology

In Lesson 8 we looked at some words derived from Greek numbers. QUADRUPLE, meaning "to increase fourfold," comes from the Latin *quad* (four). Some Latin number prefixes, with words derived from them, are given below:

uni (one) Examples: *uni*cycle, *uni*verse
duo (two) Examples: *du*plicate, *du*al
tri (three) Examples: *tri*dent, *tri*o
quad (four) Examples: *quad*rangle, *quad*ruped
quin (five) Examples: *quin*tet, *quin*tuplets
sex (six) Examples: *sex*tet, *sex*tant
sept (seven) Examples: *Sept*ember, *sept*ennial
octo (eight) Examples: *Octo*ber, *oct*et
non/nov (nine) Examples: *Nov*ember, *non*agenarian
decim (ten) Examples: *Decem*ber, *decim*ate
cent (hundred) Examples: *cent*ury, *cent*
milli (thousand) Examples: *milli*pede, *mille*nnium

ACROSS

1. not directly involved; impartial
7. plentifully supplied; filled
11. begging
12. marked by rigorous self-denial (6)
13. a state of complete political disorder
15. a monumentally large tomb
17. having to do with water; watery
18. a charm worn to guard against evil (2)
19. language peculiar to a community or class; phrase with a meaning different from its literal sense (7)
20. an overaccumulation of something
22. rotten (said of eggs)
23. morally pure
24. to remove from the record
28. a holder for burning incense
30. described in vivid detail
31. lessening the seriousness of
33. lessening the severity of without curing
34. an insult or affront to one's dignity
38. a gay and festive occasion
39. that inspires fear or respect in one
40. rough or stormy; harsh
41. a very narrow pass
43. a state of great perplexity (9)
44. very great; enormous
45. a narrow-minded, uncultured person
46. ghostlike
47. a group of personal attendants
48. a condition of slavery or bondage

DOWN

1. to dishearten completely
2. winding in and out; wavy
3. not much given to talking
4. the killing of a person as an act of mercy
5. a passing from one state or condition to another
6. a ruling group of three
8. an all-embracing view or spectacle
9. to breathe out
10. the expressing of views contrary to those held officially
14. to settle differences between persons or groups
16. to increase fourfold
20. to apply a hot iron to a wound to help healing
21. fond of being with people; sociable
25. a slang spoken by a particular group (5)
26. an expert on birds
27. of, due from, or suitable to a son or daughter
29. beneficial; healthful
32. to devise reasons to justify one's behavior
34. seeming to be less dangerous than it is
35. clumsy; awkward
36. to share in the eating or drinking of (3)
37. a long and violently angry speech or outburst
38. gambler
42. a particular skill

Chapter Five

Word List 13

ABASHED	CRASS	MERCENARY
ARBITER	DEFAME	PARSIMONIOUS
BENISON	ENNUI	PROPAGANDA
BLUFF	FUNEREAL	RETROGRESS
CANKER	IDEOLOGY	SURFEIT
COMPLAISANT	INFERNO	TUREEN

Look up the words above in your dictionary. Note that many of them have more than one meaning. When you think that you know *all* the meanings of *all* the words, go on to the exercise below.

EXERCISE 13A

From the four choices following each phrase or sentence, you are to circle the letter preceding the one that is closest in meaning to the italicized word. Where the same word appears more than once, you should note that it is being used in different senses.

1. quite *abashed*
   (a) angry (b) embarrassed (c) battered (d) surprised

2. to choose an *arbiter*
   (a) person able to act as a temporary leader (b) person able to judge or decide (c) head of a twelve-person jury (d) successor to a leader

3. to receive her *benison*
   (a) blessing (b) meat (c) support (d) offer

4. to *bluff* someone
   (a) question (b) ignore (c) stop (d) fool

5. a *bluff* manner
   (a) foolish (b) frank (c) suspicious (d) distant

6. to reach the *bluff*
   (a) small island (b) steep cliff (c) shallow stream (d) beach

7. to treat the *canker*
   (a) deep cut (b) large bruise (c) broken bone (d) spreading sore

8. a *canker* in society
   (a) unpredictable effect (b) lackadaisical attitude (c) evil influence (d) strong concern

9. a *complaisant* person
   (a) self-satisfied (b) obliging (c) lazy (d) contented

10. a *crass* remark
    (a) deliberately provocative (b) coarsely stupid (c) wittily amusing (d) unintentionally cruel

11. to *defame* someone
    (a) disprove the claim of (b) attack the reputation of (c) attempt to discourage (d) have a high opinion of

12. to overcome *ennui*
    (a) boredom (b) fault (c) handicap (d) unwillingness

13. a *funereal* manner
    (a) unhealthy (b) gloomy (c) bitter (d) formal

14. a false *ideology*
    (a) claim to the throne (b) book dealing with ideas (c) set of beliefs (d) notion not subject to proof

15. to escape from the *inferno*
    (a) sea monster (b) intense heat (c) whirlpool (d) intense cold

16. Dante's *Inferno*
    (a) heaven (b) hell (c) machine (d) monster

17. He is a *mercenary*.
    (a) hired soldier (b) hired killer (c) loyal follower (d) unfeeling person

18. They are both *mercenary*.
    (a) interested only in warfare (b) concerned only with making money (c) lacking in modesty (d) foolishly brave

19. a *parsimonious* person
    (a) scholarly (b) godly (c) miserly (d) cautious

20. attempts at *propaganda*
    (a) converting people to religion by the use of force (b) creating new plants through crossbreeding (c) creating forms of life in the laboratory (d) deliberately spreading ideas that will help one's own cause or injure an enemy's

21. to start to *retrogress*
    (a) improve (b) worsen (c) adapt (d) suffer

22. to be *surfeited*
    (a) very easily satisfied (b) given too much of something (c) worked to the point of exhaustion (d) deliberately deceived

23. a white *tureen*
    (a) dish (b) cover (c) vase (d) jug

Check your answers against the correct ones given below. The answers are not in order; this is to prevent your eye from catching sight of the correct answers before you have had a chance to do the exercise on your own.

6b. 13b. 11b. 18b. 7d. 17a. 1b. 23a. 15b. 22b. 2b. 8c. 12a. 19c. 10b. 14c. 9b. 21b. 4d. 5b. 16b. 3a. 20d.

Look up in your dictionary all the words for which you gave incorrect answers. Only when you have done this should you go on to the next exercise.

EXERCISE 13B
Each word in Word List 13 is used several times in the following sentences to illustrate different meanings or usage. One of the sentences for each word uses the italicized word incorrectly. You are to circle the letter preceding the sentence.

1. (a) She was not at all *abashed* at being found out to be a liar. (b) The slaves *abashed* themselves before their owner by touching the floor with their foreheads. (c) The children were *abashed* when they discovered I had seen them taking the cookies.

2. (a) Her skill as an *arbiter* in labor-management disputes is well known. (b) The man chosen to *arbiter* this dispute must be a person of great tact. (c) The referee is the sole *arbiter* in a boxing match. (d) That young designer became the supreme *arbiter* of what was fashionable among the wealthy set.

3. (a) Great chunks of steaming *benison* were heaped on our plates. (b) The only help they seek is the *benison* of Allah. (c) After receiving the minister's *benison*, we departed.

4. (a) That dog's bark is just a *bluff* and can safely be ignored. (b) The fort was built atop a *bluff* overlooking the river. (c) Her *bluff* and hearty manner made her a good choice as spokesperson for the group. (d) The heavy shelling from the enemy guns had made a wide *bluff* in our defenses.

5. (a) Organized crime is a *canker* that is slowly destroying the health of our society. (b) The horse must not be ridden for a while because its hoofs are *cankerous*. (c) She has a *canker* in her mouth that is not responding to treatment. (d) His *cankerous* manner makes him a very difficult person to get along with.

6. (a) After winning eight games in a row, it was natural for us to grow *complaisant*. (b) They surrounded themselves with a bunch of *complaisant* assistants. (c) The people of the house showed by their *complaisance* that I was welcome.

7. (a) Many people deplore the *crass* commercialism of large stores during the Christmas season. (b) His proposal of marriage to the grieving widow immediately after the funeral is an example of his *crassness*. (c) It will *crass* her terribly if she finds out what you have done.

8. (a) I cannot allow him to *defame* me by saying that I stole the money. (b) She called me a cheat, a liar, a thief, and other *defamatory* names. (c) If the article constitutes *defamation* of character, it may result in a suit for libel. (d) He won lasting *defame* as a man who cheated hundreds of people out of their savings.

9. (a) The audience did not conceal its *ennui* from the lecturer. (b) Father tried to entertain the children when they grew *ennui*. (c) Nothing could shake off the *ennui* that blanketed their lives.

10. (a) The undertaker was dressed in *funereal* black. (b) A deep, *funereal* gloom had descended upon the household. (c) Only six people attended the *funereal*.

11. (a) Nelson Mandela's political *ideology* remained unchanged despite his many years in prison. (b) The *ideology* of the group was not fixed but adapted itself to fit changing conditions. (c) She *ideologized* her gymnastics teacher and did everything she was told.

12. (a) A sailor discovered the *inferno* machine only minutes before it was due to go off. (b) Ten minutes after the fire started, the place was an *inferno*. (c) The boiler room was an *inferno* of heat, noise, and confusion.

13. (a) The sultan's army was composed mainly of *mercenaries* recruited in Europe. (b) With tourists flocking into the area, it is not surprising that storekeepers have become *mercenary*. (c) Heating the wax makes it *mercenary* and easy to work.

14. (a) He is so *parsimonious* that it hurts him to spend 50 cents for a newspaper. (b) Government departments are extremely *parsimonious* when it comes to giving out information. (c) In less than three months she had squandered her *parsimony*. (d) It is useless to ask them for money as their *parsimony* is well known.

15. (a) Reports of heavy losses in yesterday's fighting are simply enemy *propaganda*. (b) It is sheer *propaganda* to say that I haven't been working hard. (c) The group plans to *propagandize* for the cause of states' rights. (d) She is a *propagandist* for a variety of dubious causes.

16. (a) The wage increase was made *retrogressive* to January first. (b) Our injured dog did well at first but is now beginning to *retrogress*. (c) The country is actually *retrogressing* due to the incompetence of its ruler.

17. (a) We were *surfeited* with food at the banquet. (b) We are *surfeited* with the childish programs on television. (c) There was a *surfeit* of fine foods at the banquet. (d) The government will distribute *surfeit* foods to needy countries overseas.

18. (a) The *tureen* was filled with tomato soup. (b) The potatoes were *tureened* until they were a golden brown.

EXERCISE 13C

The word *kill* is used in each of the twelve sentences below. Sometimes it is used literally and sometimes metaphorically (explanations of these terms will be found in the Introduction). Write (L) where you think the word is used literally; write (M) where you think it is being used metaphorically.

1. They killed ( ) the rabbit with a sharp blow behind the ears.

2. She had spent the morning at the January sales, and her feet were killing ( ) her.

3. Six people were killed ( ) and fourteen wounded in yesterday's battle.

4. She killed ( ) the motor and let the boat come to a stop.

5. The Senate yesterday killed ( ) the bill to reduce import duties on automobiles.

6. The loss of our star pitcher has killed ( ) whatever chance we had of winning.

7. The cat proudly brought home a bird it had killed ( ).

8. There is no point in killing ( ) ourselves to get to the railroad station as the train will probably be late.

9. It is not true that television is killing ( ) interest in baseball.

10. Thousands of people are killed ( ) on our highways every year.

11. The front-runners in the marathon set a killing ( ) pace.

12. With sequined gowns and suits and with flowing colorful scarves, the entertainers were dressed to kill ( ).

WORDLY WISE 13

COMPLAISANT means "agreeable, obliging." This word and *complacent* (see Word List 20) are homonyms but have quite different meanings; *complacent* means "smugly self-satisfied."

ENNUI is a feeling of weariness or boredom; the word comes to us from the French and is pronounced *awn-WEE.*

Etymology

Study the root and prefixes given below, together with the English words derived from them. Capitalized words are those given in the Word List. You should look up in a dictionary any words that are unfamiliar to you.

Prefixes: *retro-* (back, backward) Latin — Examples: *RETRO*GRESS, *retro*active, *retro*spect

pro- (forward) Latin — Examples: *pro*gress, *pro*spect

Root: *merc* (pay) Latin — Examples: *MERCE*NARY, *mer*chant, com*merc*ial

Word List 14

ABLUTION	CUISINE	OGLE
BAUBLE	DEMOTE	PENURY
BESTIAL	FLUX	RAILLERY
BOMBASTIC	GARB	SCINTILLATE
CHARY	IMPECCABLE	SURVEY
CONGENITAL	INVECTIVE	VERBATIM

Look up the words above in your dictionary. Note that many of them have more than one meaning. When you think that you know *all* the meanings of *all* the words, go on to the exercise below.

EXERCISE 14A

Each word in Word List 14 is used several times in the sentences below to illustrate different meanings or usage. One of the sentences for each word uses the italicized word incorrectly. You are to circle the letter preceding the sentence.

1. daily *ablutions*
   (a) exercises   (b) washings   (c) reports
   (d) prayers

2. to accept the *bauble*
   (a) trinket   (b) compliment   (c) situation
   (d) report

3. a *bestial* manner
   (a) overrefined (b) brutal (c) inborn (d) acquired

4. a *bombastic* person
   (a) pompous (b) bold (c) modest (d) timorous

5. He seems *chary.*
   (a) stupid   (b) happy   (c) cautious   (d) despondent

6. a *congenital* disease
   (a) incurable (b) present from birth (c) likely to cause death (d) widespread

7. French *cuisine*
   (a) gallantry   (b) fashion   (c) cooking
   (d) patriotism

8. to *demote* someone
   (a) disappoint (b) reduce in rank (c) point out (d) humiliate

9. a state of *flux*
   (a) harmony (b) change (c) rest (d) grace

10. to prevent the *flux*
    (a) explosion (b) flow (c) return (d) destruction

11. Use plenty of *flux*.
    (a) substance used in removing paint (b) substance used in joining metals (c) substance used in waterproofing wood (d) substance used in hardening glue

12. strange *garb*
    (a) looks (b) manners (c) clothes (d) foods

13. *impeccable* taste
    (a) contrived (b) faultless (c) dubious (d) outlandish

14. Ignore his *invective*.
    (a) showy manner (b) boastful talk (c) self-pitying plea (d) abusive language

15. to *ogle* someone
    (a) glance flirtatiously at (b) look accusingly at (c) stare foolishly at (d) glare angrily at

16. living in *penury*
    (a) abject fear (b) great luxury (c) exotic surroundings (d) extreme poverty

17. the *raillery* of his classmates
    (a) lighthearted teasing (b) excessive flattery (c) deceitful behavior (d) empty promises

18. See it *scintillate*.
    (a) swing (b) sparkle (c) wriggle (d) revolve

19. to *survey* the area
    (a) visit (b) prefer (c) measure (d) avoid

20. to conduct a *survey*
    (a) large class (b) group of musicians (c) detailed study (d) church service

21. to *survey* someone
    (a) look down on (b) look up to (c) look closely at (d) think about

22. to repeat it *verbatim*
    (a) over and over again (b) slowly and distinctly (c) word for word (d) entirely from memory

Check your answers against the correct ones given below. The answers are not in order; this is to prevent your eye from catching sight of the correct answers before you have had a chance to do the exercise on your own.

5c. 10b. 17a. 6b. 13b. 1b. 14d. 2a. 16d. 3b. 9b. 11b. 18b. 15a. 21c. 12c. 20c. 8b. 19c. 4a. 22c. 7c.

Look up in your dictionary all the words for which you gave incorrect answers. Only when you have done this should you go on to the next exercise.

EXERCISE 14B

Each word in Word List 14 is used several times in the sentences below to illustrate different meanings or usage. One of the sentences for each word uses the *italicized* word incorrectly. You are to circle the letter preceding the sentence.

1. (a) He sat in the library in complete *ablution*. (b) After completing his *ablutions*, he dressed and came down to breakfast. (c) You may perform your *ablutions* as soon as the bathroom is free.

2. (a) She had a little *bauble* for each of the children. (b) When he saw how he had been tricked, he began to *bauble*. (c) They are so wealthy that the cars and boats they showered on their children seem mere *baubles*.

3. (a) He spoke eloquently on the *bestial* nature of war. (b) He was unused to being among civilized people and had the most *bestial* manners. (c) The deliberate *bestialities* of the conquerors are graphically described in this book. (d) The wild animals

54

are kept in a large *bestial,* open to the public every day.

4. (a) After four days of heavy *bombast* from the enemy guns, the town surrendered. (b) Her *bombastic* style of speaking was not calculated to win her many supporters. (c) Although he tries to speak simply, he cannot help sounding *bombastic.* (d) The occasional plain speech heard in the legislature stands out like an island in a vast sea of *bombast.*

5. (a) She is naturally *chary* of compliments from strangers. (b) Be more *chary* in your choice of friends. (c) He is a busy man, *chary* of his time. (d) It was a *chary* moment for us as we waited for the results to be announced.

6. (a) She seems a very *congenital* administrator, always ready with a smile and a greeting. (b) Doctors think these defects occur during childhood and are not *congenital.* (c) The man is a *congenital* liar and wouldn't recognize the truth if he heard it.

7. (a) Rich sauces are the most characteristic element in French *cuisine.* (b) The *cuisine* of the inn is a blend of American and Swedish cooking. (c) In less than ten minutes she had whipped up a delicious *cuisine* for us.

8. (a) The word "quadruped" *demotes* a four-footed animal. (b) The soldier was *demoted* from sergeant to private.

9. (a) Fashions are in a constant state of *flux.* (b) The patient's condition took a sudden *flux* for the worst. (c) The cause of the sudden *flux* of water is not known. (d) The metal surfaces to be joined are first rubbed with a *flux* such as borax or resin.

10. (a) The children spoke a strange *garb* that none of us understood. (b) She wore the solemn *garb* of an undertaker. (c) A tall woman, *garbed* in black from head to toe, came to the door.

11. (a) She has an *impeccable* record as a mediator in labor-management disputes. (b) He was *impeccably* dressed in dinner jacket and starched shirt. (c) They were *impeccable* to any criticism regarding their son's behavior. (d) The book is written in the *impeccable* style we have come to expect from this writer.

12. (a) The commanding officer issued an *invective* that no soldiers were to leave their posts. (b) He was quite unprepared for the *invective* that greeted him when he opened the door. (c) A stream of *invective* poured from her as her anger mounted.

13. (a) His role in the play called for him to do little but *ogle* the leading lady. (b) They tried to *ogle* an invitation to the party but met with no success.

14. (a) After wasting their money, the family was reduced to *penury.* (b) He kept his money in a *penury* that was guarded with a heavy lock. (c) It was impossible to save money in those *penurious* times. (d) After losing all her money, she lived *penuriously* for many years.

15. (a) Some good-natured *raillery* followed when he fell off the horse. (b) They mistake noise for gaiety and *raillery* for wit. (c) The *raillery* extends all around the house and is in good repair.

16. (a) She is a fine speaker with a *scintillating* wit. (b) Her eyes *scintillated* as she told us of her plans. (c) Brandy is a *scintillate* of carefully-chosen wines. (d) The musicians' heavily sequined jackets *scintillated* in the light.

17. (a) The message was *surveyed* to him by a trusted servant. (b) The land must be carefully *surveyed* before the purchase can be registered. (c) She *surveyed* us in a grand way and asked what we wanted. (d) The *survey* indicates a serious shortage of schools in the area.

18. (a) Included is a *verbatim* record of what was said at the meeting. (b) She's a very *verbatim*

speaker who lets twenty words do the work of five. (c) After reading the speech once, she was able to deliver it *verbatim*.

EXERCISE 14C

From the five numbered choices, complete the analogies below by underlining the word that stands in the same relationship to the third word as the second word does to the first. An explanation of analogies is given in the Introduction.

1. slavery:freedom :: anarchy: (1) master (2) warfare (3) order (4) monarchy (5) anarchic

2. diamond:costly :: bauble: (1) gem (2) expensive (3) stone (4) sparkling (5) cheap

3. imperative:command :: interrogative: (1) question (2) order (3) silence (4) answer (5) inquisitive

4. aviary:birds :: apiary: (1) apes (2) bees (3) flying (4) nests (5) honey

5. inclement:mercy :: impeccable: (1) judgment (2) fault (3) clean (4) taste (5) change

6. putrid:meat :: addled: (1) fish (2) bird (3) confused (4) rotten (5) egg

7. maladroit:clumsy :: adept: (1) backward (2) awkward (3) slow (4) skillful (5) ignorant

8. pentagon:five :: octagon: (1) seven (2) triangle (3) eight (4) circle (5) nine

9. censor:censer :: bough: (1) incense (2) tree (3) bow (4) bend (5) twig

10. four:quadruple :: two: (1) biped (2) fold (3) exact (4) double (5) pair

WORDLY WISE 14

In French, *la cuisine* is "the kitchen." CUISINE (*kwi-ZEEN*) retains the French pronunciation but means a manner of preparing food. (Each

country seems to have a distinctive *cuisine*.)

Etymology

Study the roots and prefixes given below, together with the English words derived from them. Capitalized words are those given in the Word List. You should look up in a dictionary any words that are unfamiliar to you.

Prefixes: (Review) *im-* (not) Latin — Example: IMPECCABLE

(Review) *con-* (with) Latin — Example: CONGENITAL

Roots: *pecca* (fault) Latin — Examples: IMPECCABLE, *pecca*dillo

gen (birth, family, race) Latin — Examples: CONGENITAL, *gen*ealogy, *geno*cide

---

Word List 15

ANNEAL	CULPABLE	PACIFIC
BECOMING	ENDORSE	PERNICIOUS
BIZARRE	FREEBOOTER	RETINUE
BUOYANT	HALLMARK	SCRIP
CHATTEL	INCOGNITO	SYMMETRICAL
CRANIUM	IRREVOCABLE	VERVE

Look up the words above in your dictionary. Note that many of them have more than one meaning. When you think that you know *all* the meanings of *all* the words, go on to the exercise below.

EXERCISE 15A

From the four choices following each phrase or sentence, you are to circle the letter preceding the one that is closest in meaning to the italicized word. Where the same word appears more than once, you should note that it is being used in different senses.

1. to *anneal* metal
   (a) bond together in layers (b) toughen by heating and then cooling (c) draw out into thin wire (d) beat into paper-thin leaf

2. a *becoming* manner
   (a) outrageously rude (b) grotesquely insincere (c) pleasingly suitable (d) elaborately formal

3. a *bizarre* manner
   (a) oriental   (b) fantastic   (c) ingratiating
   (d) grating

4. It is *buoyant*.
   (a) easily set on fire (b) light in weight
   (c) able to float (d) easily removable

5. a *buoyant* personality
   (a) moody (b) cheerful (c) depressed (d) un-predictable

6. a *chattel* mortgage
   (a) on movable property (b) on land and buildings (c) on personal income (d) renew-able on request.

7. a blow on the *cranium*
   (a) base of the spine (b) top of the skull
   (c) point of the jaw (d) kneecap

8. He is *culpable*.
   (a) blameworthy (b) free of guilt (c) in poor health (d) undecided

9. to *endorse* a candidate
   (a) nominate (b) oppose (c) defeat (d) ex-press support of

10. to *endorse* a check
    (a) verify the signature on (b) sign the back of (c) make a record of (d) give cash in exchange for

11. a redoubtable *freebooter*
    (a) pirate (b) runner (c) general (d) business-person

12. Look for the *hallmark*.
    (a) mark that shows high tide (b) boundary mark between countries (c) flaw in glass or china objects (d) stamp on gold or silver objects

13. the *hallmark* of a soldier
    (a) identification tag (b) periodic appraisal (c) distinguishing characteristic (d) record of service

14. to travel *incognito*
    (a) with one's identity concealed (b) without cost to oneself (c) with utmost speed (d) without any definite plan

15. an *irrevocable* decision
    (a) hasty (b) unalterable (c) momentous (d) joint

16. a *pacific* society
    (a) peaceful (b) weak (c) remote (d) primi-tive

17. a *pernicious* effect
    (a) harmful (b) permanent (c) slight (d) de-layed

18. a large *retinue*
    (a) circle of admirers (b) train of attendants (c) sum of money (d) fleet of ships

19. to receive *scrip*
    (a) forgiveness for one's sins (b) paper entitling the bearer to receive something (c) the right to enter or leave a country at will (d) wages in the form of goods rather than money

20. *symmetrical* parts
    (a) irregular   (b) balanced   (c) incomplete
    (d) detachable

21. done with *verve*
    (a) enthusiasm   (b) timidity   (c) regret
    (d) forethought

Check your answers against the correct ones given below. The answers are not in order; this is to prevent your eye from catching sight of the correct answers before you have had a chance to do the exercise on your own.

6a. 11a. 9d. 15b. 4c. 18b. 14a. 21a. 1b. 5b. 17a. 2c. 20b. 7b. 13c. 10b. 8a. 12d. 19b. 16a. 3b.

Look up in your dictionary all the words for which you gave incorrect answers. Only when you have done this should you go on to the next exercise.

Each word in Word List 15 is used several times in the sentences below to illustrate different meanings or usage. One of the sentences for each word uses the italicized word incorrectly. You are to circle the letter preceding the sentence.

1. (a) The judge may *anneal* the contract if it is proved that the facts were misrepresented. (b) They *anneal* the metal by heating it in the furnace and allowing it to cool slowly.

2. (a) Your coat is very *becoming*. (b) Students should conduct themselves in a manner *becoming* young adults. (c) With a *becoming* modesty they thanked me for the help I had given them. (d) We thought it *becoming* strange that no one saw the police leaving the inn.

3. (a) She had scored a maximum 100 points, and such a *bizarre* result had never been seen before. (b) The house was furnished in the most *bizarre* manner imaginable. (c) Trends in modern painting are becoming increasingly *bizarre*. (d) The street was as colorful and as noisy as an oriental *bizarre*.

4. (a) Sea water is more *buoyant* than fresh water. (b) They clung to the *buoyant* for dear life until they were rescued. (c) Her *buoyant* spirits never failed to cheer us when the going got tough. (d) The human body is quite *buoyant* and will float in water.

5. (a) All the goods and *chattels* were sold; the family was left with only some land and buildings. (b) She's looking for a *chattel* that she can buy cheaply. (c) You can take out a *chattel* mortgage on livestock, furniture, or your automobile.

6. (a) He was completely bald, and his *cranium* shone a waxy yellow in the dim light. (b) Surgeons cut a hole in the patient's *cranium* in order to operate on the brain. (c) A baby's *cranial* bones remain quite soft for some time after birth.

7. (a) The *culpable* negligence of the driver was a major cause of the accident. (b) Those who advocate lawlessness are as *culpable* as the lawbreakers themselves. (c) She gave a *culpable* start when I mentioned the robbery.

8. (a) The newspaper will not *endorse* either candidate in the election. (b) The bank will not cash the check unless you *endorse* it. (c) The governor has *endorsed* these new measures. (d) We need your *endorse* before we can go ahead with our plans.

9. (a) Returning visitors are allowed up to one hundred dollars *freebooter* but must pay duty on goods worth more than that amount. (b) Two hundred years ago *freebooters* roamed the Caribbean Sea, attacking innocent traders. (c) Captain Henry Morgan was an English gentleman who turned to piracy and became a notorious *freebooter*.

10. (a) The wet glass had left an unsightly *hallmark* on the tabletop. (b) The *hallmark* on this silver bowl guarantees that it is genuine. (c) The ability to fade into the background is the *hallmark* of the successful spy. (d) An unashamed isolationism was the *hallmark* of the presidency during those years.

11. (a) The young prince and princess toured the country *incognito* to learn the true feelings of the people. (b) He's one of those *incognito* persons you forget five minutes after leaving.

12. (a) She is *irrevocably* opposed to any change in the law. (b) A sentence of death, once carried out, is *irrevocable*. (c) The knot had been tied so tightly that it was *irrevocable*.

13. (a) This herb is a *pacific* for a number of ailments. (b) It is a *pacific* country and resolves disputes by discussion rather than by warfare. (c) They contrasted the *pacific* nations of Asia with war-loving Europe. (d) It was because of its calm, unruffled surface that the *Pacific* Ocean was so called.

14. (a) Television shows that glorify violence have a *pernicious* effect on young people's minds. (b) Someone had started a *pernicious* rumor to the effect that she had been fired from her job. (c) The disease is the more *pernicious* for being undetectable in its early stages. (d) The question was ruled out of order as it was not *pernicious* to the business at hand.

15. (a) Their lands brought them an annual *retinue* of five thousand dollars. (b) The bishop, followed by a *retinue* of priests and altar boys, proceeded down the aisle. (c) The larger a duke's *retinue,* the more important was he believed to be.

16. (a) When coins were in short supply, *scrip* was used for amounts under one dollar. (b) The people received *scrip,* which they could exchange for goods and services. (c) Some of the letters were in printed capitals, others were in *scrip.*

17. (a) The human body in outline is roughly *symmetrical.* (b) After fluttering violently, her heartbeat became *symmetrical* again. (c) The plants had been arranged so *symmetrically* that the garden looked artificial.

18. (a) She plays tennis with the *verve* of someone half her age. (b) The figures are drawn in so distorted a manner that they *verve* on the grotesque. (c) The animals are drawn with such *verve* that they seem about to leap off the paper.

EXERCISE 15C

This exercise combines synonyms and antonyms. You are to underline the word which is *either* most similar in meaning *or* most nearly opposite in meaning to the CAPITALIZED word. Underline only one word for each question after deciding that it is *either* an antonym *or* a synonym, and write A (for antonym) or S (for synonym) after the capitalized word. Allow only fifteen minutes for this test. If you cannot answer a question, go on to the next one without delay. If you have time left over at the end, go back and try to fill in unanswered questions.

26 or over correct: excellent
22 to 25 correct: good
21 or under correct: thorough review of A exercises indicated

1. EMBARRASSED . . . . .
becoming abashed verbatim culpable blatant

2. UNSUITABLE . . . . .
bestial funereal becoming pernicious chary

3. DRESS . . . . .
garb flux impeccable crass bluff

4. GLOOMY . . . . .
impeccable parsimonious buoyant crass pernicious

5. ORDINARY . . . . .
congenital bombastic incognito bizarre resilient

6. TRINKET . . . . .
gala bauble chattel raillery benison

7. INNOCENT . . . . .
discursive reticent disinterested culpable literate

8. GENEROUS . . . . .
resilient expository extenuating chaste parsimonious

9. TURBULENT . . . . .
impeccable mercenary crass complaisant pacific

10. EXTOL . . . . .
defame cremate exhale survey partake

11. HARMLESS . . . . .
overwrought inveterate pernicious grueling strategic

12. PAUCITY . . . . .
species surfeit choler canker chattel

13. BALANCED .....
ambidextrous inopportune ambivalence symmetrical discursive

14. BLESSING .....
ideology bauble stamina sinecure benison

15. ENTHUSIASM .....
verve inferno bluff hallmark scrip

16. SPOTLESS .....
glutinous impeccable gregarious bombastic salutary

17. PROGRESS .....
proclivity ennui gregarious heresy retrogress

18. LOQUACIOUS .....
literate inveterate impeccable reticent verbatim

19. VULGAR .....
whimsical scrip crass flux addled

20. MONOTONY .....
tedium raillery homily forte stalemate

21. EXCITEMENT .....
invective ennui surfeit choler indignity

22. ADEPT .....
abashed culpable maladroit irrational inherent

23. POVERTY .....
penury paucity anarchy proclivity indignity

24. OBLIGING .....
infatuated parsimonious mercenary complaisant pernicious

25. HABITUAL .....
becoming inveterate culpable verbatim imperative

26. CHANGE .....
mediate scrip surfeit ennui flux

27. FRANK .....
inherent primordial bluff prodigious crass

28. DISCREET .....
impious blatant impeccable buoyant bizarre

29. SPARKLE .....
expunge anneal ogle scintillate flux

30. WARY .....
complaisant discursive wayward chary abashed

WORDLY WISE 15

BIZARRE means "strikingly out of the ordinary." A *bazaar* is a market or other place where goods are sold. These two words are pronounced the same.

The CRANIUM is the bone structure that encloses and protects the brain; the *skull* is the name given to the entire bone structure of the head, including the teeth and jawbone.

Etymology

Study the roots and prefixes given below, together with the English words derived from them. Capitalized words are those given in the Word List. You should look up in a dictionary any words that are unfamiliar to you.

Prefixes: *en-* (on) Latin – Examples: *EN*DORSE, *en*throne

sym- (with, together) Greek – Examples: *SYM*METRICAL, *sym*pathy

Roots: *dors* (back) Latin – Examples: EN*DORSE*, *dors*al

metr (measure) Greek – Examples: SYM*METR*ICAL, *METR*ONOME

ACROSS

1. abusive language
4. a high, steep cliff or bank
6. using pompous and inflated language
12. unwilling to spend money; miserly
14. a feeling of weariness or boredom
15. the part of the skull enclosing the brain
16. deserving of blame
18. a large, deep, covered dish
20. a set of beliefs of a person or group
22. to glance at flirtatiously or impertinently
23. brutal or cruel like a beast
26. to sparkle or twinkle
28. a sign that something is genuine
30. style of dressing; clothing
32. to attack the reputation of
33. a condition of extreme poverty
35. present from birth; inborn
36. authority to act for another (4)
37. coarsely stupid
39. made ill at ease; embarrassed
41. lighthearted teasing
42. of a quiet, peaceful nature
44. a washing of the body
48. that cannot be undone or changed
50. plant fiber used for rope (8)
51. hell or a place resembling hell
52. to move backward to a worse condition
53. a train of attendants
54. to look over carefully
55. to make valid by signing the back of
56. a condition of change

DOWN

1. without fault or error
2. in exactly the same words
3. style or manner of cooking
4. a cheap piece of jewelry or finery
5. a pirate; a buccaneer
7. a drug derived from opium (1)
8. strikingly out of the ordinary; fantastic
9. to give too much of something
10. a piece of property that can be moved
11. to toughen (metal) by heating, then cooling
13. with one's identity concealed
17. the deliberate spreading of usually false ideas
19. a spreading sore; an evil influence
21. a pointed, two-edged surgeon's knife (6)
24. having a balanced or harmonious arrangement
25. willful; disobedient (8)
27. cautious; not taking chances
29. suitable in appearance; seemly
31. a blessing
34. able to float; able to rise in air
35. anxious to please; obliging
36. causing harm; destructive
38. interested only in making money
40. paper entitling the bearer to receive something
43. gloomy; solemn
45. a jailer (3)
46. one able to judge or decide
47. to put in a lower grade or rank
49. great enthusiasm or spirit

Chapter Six

Word List 16

AFFIRM	FRANCHISE	PREDICAMENT
AVARICE	HERALD	SANCTIMONIOUS
COURSER	INSTANTANEOUS	STEVEDORE
DEVOTEE	MARATHON	THRONG
DOSSIER	METTLE	UNREMITTING
EXONERATE		

Look up the words above in your dictionary. Note that many of them have more than one meaning. When you think that you know *all* the meanings of *all* the words, go on to the exercise below.

EXERCISE 16A

From the four choices following each phrase or sentence, you are to circle the letter preceding the one that is closest in meaning to the italicized word. Where the same word appears more than once, you should note that it is being used in different senses.

1. to *affirm* something
   (a) deny (b) assert (c) prove (d) ignore

2. their *avarice*
   (a) greed for money (b) unbridled ambition (c) habit of overeating (d) deliberate cruelty

3. a proud *courser*
   (a) athlete (b) soldier (c) ship (d) horse

4. a *devotee* of the great dancer
   (a) bitter enemy (b) ardent supporter (c) unbiased biographer (d) direct descendant

5. a complete *dossier*
   (a) collection of documents giving a detailed report (b) set of books by a single author (c) investigation into an accident (d) failure to take proper measures

6. to *exonerate* someone
   (a) find guilty (b) declare blameless (c) re-

store to a former position (d) drive out by force

7. to receive a *franchise*
   (a) right granted by a government or a company (b) full pardon for a crime (c) summons to appear in court (d) sum of money offered as an inducement to tell what one knows

8. to extend the *franchise*
   (a) boundary of a city (b) right to vote (c) legal age for drinking, driving, etc. (d) rule of law

9. to *herald* the arrival
   (a) fear (b) announce (c) foreshadow (d) prevent

10. an *instantaneous* response
    (a) startled (b) delayed (c) immediate (d) enthusiastic

11. a *marathon* session
    (a) uninterrupted (b) secret (c) final (d) prolonged

12. to enter the *marathon*
    (a) footrace of about 6 miles (b) footrace of about 16 miles (c) footrace of about 26 miles (d) footrace of about 36 miles

13. to prove one's *mettle*
    (a) trust (b) spirit (c) loyalty (d) ability

14. What a *predicament*!
    (a) difficult choice (b) trying situation (c) dazzling array (d) unexpected development

15. a *sanctimonious* speech
    (a) deeply religious (b) morally uplifting (c) rousingly patriotic (d) falsely pious

16. They are *stevedores*.

(a) dockworkers (b) millworkers (c) mine-workers (d) farmworkers

17. a great *throng*
    (a) crowd of people (b) angry outburst (c) cry of greeting (d) display of strength

18. *unremitting* toil
    (a) unrewarding (b) undignified (c) unending (d) unhurried

Check your answers against the correct ones given below. The answers are not in order; this is to prevent your eye from catching sight of the correct answers before you have had a chance to do the exercise on your own.

6b. 11d. 9b. 15d. 4b. 18c. 14b. 1b. 5a. 2a. 7a. 13b. 10c. 8b. 12c. 16a. 3d. 17a.

Look up in your dictionary all the words for which you gave incorrect answers. Only when you have done this should you go on to the next exercise.

EXERCISE 16B

Each word in Word List 16 is used several times in the sentences below to illustrate different meanings or usage. One of the sentences for each word uses the italicized word incorrectly. You are to circle the letter preceding the sentence.

1. (a) A witness without a religion may *affirm* that his testimony is true and need not swear it under oath. (b) She will neither *affirm* the truth of the statement nor deny its falsity. (c) Humans' willingness to die for their beliefs is an *affirmation* of their nobility. (d) All ambassadorial appointments are subject to *affirmation* by the Congress.

2. (a) He was a grasping, *avaricious* old man who thought only of ways to make more money. (b) By the time she was thirty she had an *avarice* of over a million dollars. (c) So great was his *avarice* that he would never stop trying to make more money.

3. (a) She untethered the horse and allowed it to *courser* around the field. (b) The young people mounted their *coursers* and left at a gallop.

4. (a) She promised to *devotee* her life to helping the poor. (b) He has lost the support of all but his most loyal *devotees*. (c) She is a *devotee* of Eastern religions and has spent many years in India.

5. (a) A full *dossier* is kept on each patient on the pediatric floor. (b) The police must *dossier* arrested persons immediately following their indictment. (c) Before beginning her novel she built up an extensive *dossier* on Colonial American dress, language, and customs.

6. (a) The judge asked to be *exonerated* from the case as the defendant was a close friend. (b) The prisoner was *exonerated* when he proved he was elsewhere at the time the crime was committed. (c) It was demonstrated that the accident was caused by a mechanical failure, and the driver was *exonerated*.

7. (a) A bill to give sixteen-year-olds the *franchise* was defeated in the legislature today. (b) One must obtain a *franchise* from the federal government to operate a radio station. (c) Only companies granted a *franchise* from the manufacturer can sell this product. (d) She won the election by a *franchise* of over a million votes.

8. (a) We *heralded* to them as we were leaving, but they didn't see us. (b) A loud outburst of cheering *heralded* the arrival of the movie star. (c) A *herald* appeared and announced the arrival of the king and queen. (d) "It was the lark, the *herald* of the morn."

9. (a) Since the car crashed while going ninety miles an hour, death must have been *instantaneous* for the driver. (b) She got an *instantaneous* response when she called for volunteers. (c) Space travel to other galaxies seems unlikely because of the *instantaneous* distances involved.

10. (a) The *marathon* is the most exhausting event in the modern Olympics. (b) Dance *marathons*, in which the participants danced until exhausted, were once common. (c) A whale of *marathon* size was washed up on the beach in last night's storm. (d) The governor's right hand was bruised following yesterday's *marathon* of handshaking.

11. (a) There is nothing like mountain climbing to test a person's *mettle*. (b) The horse was a strong, *mettlesome* animal that needed careful handling. (c) The box was made of a gray *mettle*, and we were unable to break it open. (d) The likelihood of our being suddenly asked a question put us all on our *mettle*.

12. (a) He *predicamented* trouble for the boys if they went ahead with their plan. (b) When she saw my *predicament*, she promised to try to help me. (c) Although I want to help, I can do so only by neglecting my duties; do you see my *predicament*?

13. (a) Clad in *sanctimonious* purple and gold, the priest raised aloft the jeweled cross. (b) She quickly dropped her *sanctimonious* manner when she saw I hadn't been fooled. (c) She is a very religious person, without a trace of *sanctimoniousness* in her. (d) It annoys me to hear men who have gotten rich on war preparations talk *sanctimonious* rubbish about patriotism.

14. (a) He had been a *stevedore* all his life and enjoyed the work of unloading ships. (b) They made a little money *stevedoring* whenever help was needed down at the docks. (c) The ship struck a rock and was badly *stevedored* just below the waterline.

15. (a) Thousands of people *thronged* to see the parade. (b) A *throng* of confused ideas buzzed in his brain. (c) The loud *thronging* of the fire bell suddenly awakened her. (d) A vast *throng* had gathered to see the execution of the highwayman.

16. (a) A life of *unremitting* toil was the lot of the pioneer who went west. (b) Because of the *unremitting* circumstances, his sentence was reduced from five years to two. (c) No one has given more careful or more *unremitting* attention to the problem than I.

EXERCISE 16C

In 490 B.C. near the Greek town of Marathon, the Greeks defeated the Persians in a great battle. Following the victory, a messenger set out on foot for Athens, some twenty-six miles away. He collapsed exhausted on his arrival in Athens, but not before he had gasped out the good news. Our word MARATHON, which means (1) "a foot race run over 26 miles, 385 yards," (2) "an event requiring great stamina," and (3) "marked by an unusual length of time," commemorates the great feat of this runner.

In a manner similar to that given above for the word "marathon," describe the origin of, and the story behind, the following words:

PASTEURIZE (Word List 6) ....

....

....

MAUSOLEUM (Word List 10) ....

....

....

BOMBASTIC (Word List 14) ....

....

....

HALLMARK (Word List 15) ....

....

....

SABOTAGE (Word List 6) ....

WORDLY WISE 16

DEVOTEE is pronounced *DEV-oh-tay* or *DEV-oh-tee*.

STEVEDORE and *longshoreman* are used interchangeably by most people. Workers on the waterfront, however, are aware that a *longshoreman* is a laborer and an employee of the *stevedore*.

Etymology

Study the roots and prefixes given below, together with the English words derived from them. Capitalized words are those given in the Word List. You should look up in a dictionary any words that are unfamiliar to you.

Prefixes: *ad-, af-* (to) Latin — Examples: *AF-FIRM*, *af*flict, *ad*monish

ex- (out) Latin — Example: *EX*ONER-ATE

Roots: *onera* (load) Latin — Examples: EX-*ONER*ATE, *oner*ous

mitt or *miss* (send) Latin — Examples: UNRE*MITT*ING, trans*miss*ion

Word List 17

ANNUITY	GERMINATE	RECESSION
BEDEVILED	HETEROGENEOUS	SOJOURN
DECORUM	JETTISON	STICKLER
DIVERS	MELODRAMA	TRAVESTY
ELEMENTAL	OCULAR	VENDETTA
EXTANT	PARTIALITY	

Look up the words above in your dictionary. Note that many of them have more than one meaning. When you think that you know *all* the meanings of *all* the words, go on to the exercise below.

EXERCISE 17A

From the four choices following each phrase or sentence, you are to circle the letter preceding the one that is closest in meaning to the italicized word. Where the same word appears more than once, you should note that it is being used in different senses.

1. to receive an *annuity*
   (a) fixed yearly payment (b) increase in salary (c) final payment (d) demand for payment of taxes

2. *bedeviled* by someone
   (a) ignored (b) bewitched (c) tormented (d) flattered

3. to do it with *decorum*
   (a) unseemly haste (b) correctness and good taste (c) an air of finality (d) shocking disregard for what is proper

4. *divers* offers
   (a) various (b) similar (c) free (d) not what they seem

5. *elemental* forces
   (a) having to do with a god or gods (b) having to do with great forces of nature (c) having an unknown cause (d) that can be represented diagrammatically

6. The book is *extant*.
   (a) banned (b) lost without trace (c) still in existence (d) printed secretly

7. It will *germinate*.
   (a) become infected (b) kill bacteria (c) come to an end (d) begin to develop

8. *heterogeneous* groups
   (a) identical (b) dissimilar (c) hostile (d) changing

9. to *jettison* the cargo
   (a) take aboard (b) throw overboard (c) seize (d) fasten down

10. to watch a *melodrama*
    (a) unrealistic play in which good and evil are exaggerated (b) humorous play with much slapstick and buffoonery (c) historical play that covers many years (d) dramatic reenactment of an historical event

11. an *ocular* examination
    (a) final (b) eye (c) periodic (d) complete

12. a strong *partiality*
(a) liking (b) deterrent (c) hatred (d) constitution

13. a slow *recession*
(a) musical movement (b) funeral march (c) advance (d) moving backward

14. a pleasant *sojourn*
(a) climate (b) meal (c) manner (d) stay

15. a *stickler* for discipline
(a) thick cane used to administer beatings (b) set of rules used as a guideline (c) person who makes strict demands (d) book in which punishments are recorded

16. a *travesty* of justice
(a) instructive example (b) crude and mocking imitation (c) strict enforcer (d) unchanging rule

17. a bitter *vendetta*
(a) duel (b) feud (c) oath (d) medicine

Check your answers against the correct ones given below. The answers are not in order; this is to prevent your eye from catching sight of the correct answers before you have had a chance to do the exercise on your own.

6c. 11b. 9b. 15c. 4a. 14d. 1a. 5b. 17b. 2c. 7d. 13d. 10a. 8b. 12a. 16b. 3b.

Look up in your dictionary all the words for which you gave incorrect answers. Only when you have done this should you go on to the next exercise.

EXERCISE 17B

Each word in Word List 17 is used several times in the following sentences to illustrate different meanings or usage. One of the sentences for each word uses the italicized word incorrectly. You are to circle the letter preceding the sentence.

1. (a) The land will be held by his family in *annuity* as long as the taxes are paid on it. (b) She bought an *annuity* which brings her $4,000 a year. (c) He receives an *annuity* of $2,000 a year from the trust fund set up by his mother.

2. (a) The industry has been *bedeviled* by strikes and lockouts for the past few years. (b) The poor woman is *bedeviled* by creditors and has no way of paying them off. (c) He *bedeviled* the eggs and arranged them tastefully on a large platter.

3. (a) The proceedings were conducted with great *decorum*. (b) The *decorum* of the restaurant was a mixture of French Provincial and Early American. (c) Her *decorum* on the public platform earned her the respect of her listeners.

4. (a) The president listened to a *divers* range of opinions before deciding. (b) We listened to *divers* opinions as to what we ought to do. (c) There are, of course, *divers* musical styles, and she is familiar with them all.

5. (a) The problem is a very *elemental* one that you should have no difficulty in solving. (b) All night the storm raged with *elemental* fury. (c) The rains beat down with *elemental* force. (d) Whitman's poetry has a wild and *elemental* quality that impresses me greatly.

6. (a) This note, supposedly written by him, must be a forgery as none of his letters are *extant*. (b) This is the oldest printed Bible *extant*. (c) Cornish was once the language of Southwest England, but it is now *extant*.

7. (a) The warm spring days cause the seeds to *germinate*. (b) A strange idea was *germinating* in her brain. (c) *Germination* begins as soon as the seed coat is broken. (d) The wound had been *germinated* with a strong disinfectant.

8. (a) The book is a *heterogeneous* collection of writings on a variety of subjects. (b) The population of the United States is extremely *heterogeneous*, containing as it does people

from every nation on earth. (c) The army was no tightly disciplined body, but a *heterogeneous* collection of clerks, farmers, and shopkeepers. (d) She's a very *heterogeneous* person who can do almost anything.

9. (a) She makes a good living picking up *jettison* that has been washed up on the beach. (b) The plane *jettisoned* its fuel tanks as soon as they were empty. (c) A captain should *jettison* the cargo only if the ship is in grave distress. (d) Her willingness to *jettison* a good idea that proves unworkable is what impressed me most about her.

10. (a) In the old-fashioned *melodramas* the audience cheers the hero and boos the villain. (b) He commented on the great love that nineteenth century audiences had for *melodrama*. (c) She pointed to the door and very *melodramatically* ordered him never to darken her doorstep again. (d) She likes to *melodrama* her illness by claiming it to be malaria picked up while she was in the tropics.

11. (a) The *ocular* examination reveals that she needs reading glasses. (b) A person who loses an eye may be fitted with a false *ocular* that matches the real eye perfectly. (c) If the *ocular* muscles do not function properly, the eye may turn inward.

12. (a) "I have an almost excessive *partiality* for old china." (b) A judge must not show *partiality* in selecting the winner of the contest. (c) He has a *partiality* for cold roast beef washed down with old ale. (d) By the time she died she had completed only a small *partiality* of her vast project.

13. (a) By taxation and other measures the government hopes to avoid a business *recession*. (b) The surgeon made a five-inch *recession* just below the patient's rib cage. (c) The news of severe defeats for our armies was accompanied by a *recession* of optimism at home.

14. (a) We *sojourned* in Italy for the winter.

(b) After a most enjoyable *sojourn* in the mountains we continued our journey. (c) After being away for three months, the two *sojourns* returned looking tanned and fit.

15. (a) She is a *stickler* for following rules. (b) He would *stickle* each report on a large spike as he finished reading it.

16. (a) This blatant buying and selling of votes makes a *travesty* of democracy. (b) "We'll give her a fair trial before we string her up," said the judge, making a *travesty* of the trial. (c) This very funny book *travesties* all the great American writers of the last century. (d) He grew more and more *travesty* as he got older.

17. (a) For years she waged a *vendetta* against the family of the man who had killed her brother. (b) The *vendetta* had been going on for so long that neither family remembered how it had begun. (c) Someone had stuck a *vendetta* in his back and left him for dead in the piazza.

EXERCISE 17C

In each of the sentences below a word is omitted. From the four words provided, select the one that best completes the sentence. Allow ten minutes for this test. If you cannot answer a question, go on to the next one without delay. If you have time left over at the end, go back and try to fill in unanswered questions.

18 or over correct:	excellent
14 to 17 correct:	good
13 or under correct:	thorough review of A exercises indicated

1. They are very . . . . and let you do just as you please.
sanctimonious   redoubtable   complaisant
blatant

2. He is a . . . . of polo and owns five ponies.
courser stickler minion devotee

3. They .... the metal by heating it and allowing it to cool slowly.
   inferno flux anneal hallmark

4. The police have compiled a(n) .... on the suspect in the case.
   dossier chattel autopsy curfew

5. She took out a .... mortgage on her furniture.
   chattel filial tariff quadruple

6. The Nazi .... was repugnant to all decent people.
   ideology cuisine franchise annuity

7. She rides with such .... that I'm sure she'll win first prize at the horse show.
   verve compunction ambivalence proclivity

8. Because of the shortage of money, ... was issued which could be exchanged for goods.
   benison crass scrip annuity

9. The newspaper has not yet decided which candidate it will .... in the primary.
   endorse fathom debut exhale

10. Just minutes after the fire started, the barn was a(n) ....
    vendetta travesty inferno mendicant

11. The king, mounted on his spirited ...., led his soldiers into battle.
    courser vendetta bestial choler

12. The lovely crocuses .... the arrival of spring.
    herald interpolate expound scintillate

13. The people here are very .... and think of nothing but making money.
    mercenary imperative expository congenital

14. The townspeople .... the streets during carnival time.
    crass surfeit throng flux

15. This boxer has proved his .... by winning all of his last ten fights.
    invective progenitor mettle sinecure

16. She's a good sprinter, but she lacks the .... for the mile.
    stamina proxy quandary stipend

17. He is .... by people asking for favors.
    relegated exonerated bedeviled dismantled

18. They will .... the sea captain's body and scatter the ashes on the waves.
    expound anneal cauterize cremate

19. In former times, surgeons would .... wounds by applying hot irons to them.
    cauterize incapacitate pasteurize mettle

20. Martin Luther was charged with .... when he questioned the Church's teachings.
    propaganda heresy partiality ideology

WORDLY WISE 17

DIVERS is an old-fashioned, literary word that means "various" or "several." (He received *divers* offers.) *Diverse* means "unlike" or "different." (The ways of Europe and America are quite *diverse*.)

ELEMENTAL pertains to the four elements of air, earth, fire, and water, and is generally used to refer to great forces in nature (the *elemental* fury of the hurricane). *Elementary* means "introductory" or "simple" (*elementary* schools; an *elementary* problem).

HETEROGENEOUS means "mixed." Its antonym is *homogeneous*. (A *heterogeneous* group is a mixed group; *homogenized* milk is the same throughout.)

Etymology

Study the following roots, together with

the English words derived from them. Capitalized words are those given in the Word List. You should look up in a dictionary any words that are unfamiliar to you.

Roots: *hetero* (other) Greek — Examples: *HETERO*GENEOUS, *hetero*dox

homo (same) Greek — Examples: *homo*geneous, *homo*nym

gen (type) Greek — Examples: HETER-O*GENE*OUS, homo*gene*ous

Word List 18

AUTONOMOUS	GOURMET	PRATE
BELLIGERENT	HINDMOST	RESIDUE
DEFAULT	MANIA	SPORADIC
DOGGED	MEMOIRS	THERMAL
EMANCIPATE	OPULENCE	UMBER
FLORA		

Look up the words above in your dictionary. Note that many of them have more than one meaning. When you think that you know *all* the meanings of *all* the words, go on to the exercise below.

EXERCISE 18A

From the four choices following each phrase or sentence, you are to circle the letter preceding the one that is closest in meaning to the italicized word. Where the same word appears more than once, you should note that it is being used in different senses.

1. an *autonomous* division
   (a) self-governing (b) single (c) subsidiary (d) minor

2. a *belligerent* attitude
   (a) hostile (b) neutral (c) prejudiced (d) friendly

3. a meeting of the *belligerents*
   (a) partners in an enterprise (b) beneficiaries under a will (c) nations at war (d) neutral nations

4. to *default* on a debt
   (a) fail to make payment (b) demand payment (c) arrange payments (d) pay off

5. *dogged* efforts
   (a) determined (b) ill-fated (c) useless (d) halfhearted

6. to *emancipate* them
   (a) fail (b) understand (c) free (d) encourage

7. the *flora* of Alaska
   (a) outline (b) animals (c) people (d) plants

8. They are *gourmets*.
   (a) people who eat to excess (b) experts on fine foods (c) people devoted to exercise (d) rude, overbearing persons

9. the *hindmost* position
   (a) most exposed (b) most carefully prepared (c) farthest back (d) most convenient

10. a *mania* for something
    (a) feeling of complete indifference (b) deep love (c) bitter hostility (d) excessive enthusiasm

11. the *memoirs* of a president
    (a) collected letters (b) autobiography (c) objects associated with the career (d) stories most frequently told

12. We marveled at her *opulence*.
    (a) wealth (b) nerve (c) strength (d) skill

13. to *prate* of their wealth
    (a) talk foolishly (b) demand proof (c) say nothing (d) be jealous

14. the *residue* of the money
    (a) forfeiting (b) remainder (c) total amount (d) payment

15. *sporadic* attempts
    (a) continuous (b) unsuccessful (c) carefully timed (d) irregularly occurring

16. *thermal* properties
    (a) having to do with heat (b) having to do with light (c) having to do with sound (d) having to do with motion

17. raw *umber*

(a) marble used in sculpture (b) earth color used in artists' paints (c) sugar from cane or beet (d) cotton before it has been processed

Check your answers against the correct ones given below. The answers are not in order; this is to prevent your eye from catching sight of the correct answers before you have had a chance to do the exercise on your own.

6c. 11b. 9c. 15d. 4a. 14b. 1a. 5a. 17b. 2a. 7d. 13a. 10d. 8b. 12a. 16a. 3c.

Look up in your dictionary all the words for which you gave incorrect answers. Only when you have done this should you go on to the next exercise.

EXERCISE 18B

Each word in Word List 18 is used several times in the sentences below to illustrate different meanings or usage. One of the sentences for each word uses the italicized word incorrectly. You are to circle the letter preceding the sentence.

1. (a) The colony is *autonomous* except for the conduct of foreign affairs. (b) The student government is quite *autonomous* and is not interfered with in any way by the university administration. (c) The poem was written *autonomously*, and there have been theories as to the identity of its author.

2. (a) She's a very *belligerent* person, always looking for a fight. (b) The *belligerents* resumed the war following the breakdown of peace talks. (c) "Anyone who disagrees with me can expect a fight," he said *belligerently*. (d) The wound had been left unattended, and as a result had grown swollen and *belligerent*.

3. (a) The judges *defaulted* the jockey for deliberately obstructing other horses in the race. (b) She *defaulted* on her monthly payments and left town. (c) Since the other team failed to show up, we won by *default*. (d) In *default* of evidence, there was no trial.

4. (a) His *dogged* determination was a large factor in his success. (b) She stuck *doggedly* to her idea despite the ridicule of her listeners. (c) He's had nothing but bad luck and says he leads a *dogged* life.

5. (a) Lincoln's *Emancipation* Proclamation freed all the slaves of the Union. (b) She had *emancipated* herself from her parents' control and made decisions for herself. (c) Universal education will *emancipate* humankind from the shackles of ignorance. (d) The noise seemed to *emancipate* from a large box in the corner.

6. (a) They planted a bed of *flora* in one corner of their large vegetable garden. (b) There are over nine hundred plants on this list of the *flora* of the region. (c) He returned from his Arctic expedition with many examples of the *flora* he had found there.

7. (a) She is a *gourmet* and has paid particular attention to the regional dishes of France. (b) Braised filet of beef stuffed with truffles is a favorite dish of *gourmets*. (c) He liked to *gourmet* himself on the food until he could barely rise from the table.

8. (a) The cheering crowd followed behind the *hindmost* float in the parade. (b) She stationed herself in the *hindmost* rank, believing that she would be less likely to be noticed there. (c) Eleven o'clock was the *hindmost* hour for returning to the army base.

9. (a) He has a *mania* for sports cars and spends all his money on them. (b) For a time the game of bingo was a national *mania*. (c) People who are deprived of companionship grow *mania* and depressed.

10. (a) She devoted the last five years of her life to the writing of her *memoirs*. (b) His earliest *memoirs* are of his visits to the country at the age of four. (c) Volume I of the *memoirs* covers the period 1920 to 1941. (d) She gave orders that her *memoirs* were not to be published until twenty-five years after her death.

11. (a) Music of the seventeenth century has an *opulence* that is perhaps too rich for the taste of most people. (b) He lived a life of such *opulence* as an Indian prince might envy. (c) No expense had been spared to make the estate the most *opulent* in the neighborhood. (d) She regarded the object with such *opulence* that I ordered it removed.

12. (a) I let him *prate* on about how clever he was because it seemed to make him happy. (b) She got into a number of harmless *prates* while at school, but was never in any serious trouble. (c) He loves to *prate* of all the famous people he has known.

13. (a) A *residue* of ashes remained after the bonfire had been burned. (b) She left $5,000 to each of her children with the *residue* of the estate going to her husband. (c) They had been *residues* of the area for a number of years.

14. (a) He gave a *sporadic* wave of his hand when he saw us enter the cafe. (b) Fighting had ended along the front except for *sporadic* outbursts of gunfire. (c) *Sporadic* attempts have been made to win back the cup, but there has been no sustained effort.

15. (a) The *thermal* waters of the spa have a constant temperature of 100° F or almost 35° C. (b) A *thermal* layer of air hung over the city causing thick fog. (c) Gliders can rise hundreds of feet on *thermals,* as rising bodies of warm air are called. (d) After being swathed in heavy blankets, she soon grew *thermal* again.

16. (a) *Umber* is favored by artists as a pigment because its rich earth color is permanent. (b) Raw *umber* is a yellow-brown earth color. (c) Burnt *umber* is a reddish-brown earth color. (d) The children were in an *umber* mood when I spoke to them.

EXERCISE 18C

This exercise combines synonyms and antonyms. You are to underline the word which is *either* most similar in meaning *or* most nearly opposite in meaning to the CAPITALIZED word. Underline only one word for each question after deciding that it is *either* an antonym *or* a synonym, and write A (for antonym) or S (for synonym) after the capitalized word. Allow only fifteen minutes for this test. If you cannot answer a question, go on to the next one without delay. If you have time left over at the end, go back and try to fill in unanswered questions.

26 or over correct: excellent
22 to 25 correct: good
21 or under correct: thorough review of A exercises indicated

1. PACIFIC . . . . .
   blatant facsimile belligerent strategic ulterior

2. SUBORDINATE . . . . .
   impious discursive buoyant salutary autonomous

3. MOCKERY . . . . .
   homily travesty quandary mania ennui

4. UNENDING . . . . .
   untenable unwitting unremitting inveterate inopportune

5. LOUD . . . . .
   ire verve waft flora forte

6. FRONT . . . . .
   curfew hindmost residue relegate curtail

7. EMBARRASS . . . . .
   exploit rebut instill disconcert harangue

8. STEED . . . . .
   scapegoat lionize courser amulet filial

9. STAY . . . . .
   sojourn debut survey anneal exonerate

10. EMPTY . . . . .
    blatant inveterate expository incognito replete

11. DETERMINED . . . . .
parsimonious dogged verbatim salutary maladroit

12. ORDER . . . . .
supplant acme idiom anarchy retinue

13. FEUD . . . . .
scuttle collusion stalemate bluff vendetta

14. REMAINDER . . . . .
revelry raillery residue paucity surfeit

15. IRE . . . . .
flux idiom choler indignity thrall

16. PENURY . . . . .
canker choler ocular opiate opulence

17. GREED . . . . .
avarice decorum prate penury surfeit

18. CROWD . . . . .
paean forte throng gala scrip

19. ENSLAVE . . . . .
lionize sojourn demote emancipate endorse

20. BLAME . . . . .
gesticulate dismantle harangue anneal exonerate

21. DENY . . . . .
supplant affirm default sojourn bluff

22. SEVERAL . . . . .
wayward species divers replete fractious

23. BEGGING . . . . .
mendicant minion magnitude mediate salutary

24. DISSIMILAR . . . . .
inveterate heterogeneous parsimonious impious irrational

25. EXCESS . . . .
benison stipend surfeit invective heresy

26. REGULAR . . . .
literate complaisant sporadic verbatim instantaneous

27. INTOLERANT . . . . .
inopportune complaisant inveterate ambidextrous ulterior

28. FONDNESS . . . . .
avarice partiality surfeit penury ambivalence

29. SPIRIT . . . . .
paean cuisine stipend mettle proxy

30. EXISTING . . . . .
extant discursive resilient temperate verbatim

WORDLY WISE 18

DOGGED, meaning "determined," is an adjective and is pronounced *DOG-id* (*dogged* devotion). *Dogged* is also the past participle of the verb *to dog*, meaning "to follow closely" (*dogged* by misfortune) and in this meaning is pronounced *dog'd*.

FLORA is the name given to all the plant life of a region (the *flora* of California). This word is usually linked with *fauna*, the name given to all the animal life of a region. Sometimes these terms are confused with each other.

A GOURMET (pronounced *goor-may*) is a connoisseur of fine foods; such a person does not necessarily eat large quantities of food. A *gourmand* (pronounced *GOOR-mənd*) is also an expert on fine foods and shows this appreciation by consuming large quantities. Thus, *gourmand* has a suggestion of gluttony about it, while *gourmet* does not have this association. Both words, of course, come to us from the French.

Etymology

Study the roots given below, together with the English words derived from them. Capitalized words are those given in the Word List. You should look up in a dictionary any words that are unfamiliar to you.

Roots: *auto* (self) Greek — Examples: *AUTO-* NOMOUS, *auto*matic, *auto*mobile

belli (war) Latin — Examples: *BEL-LIGERENT*, *belli*cose, ante-*bellum*

ACROSS

1. to visit and stay for a while
4. to start developing; to sprout
8. correctness and good taste in conduct
13. differing one from another; dissimilar
15. to talk foolishly and boastfully
17. a yellowish-brown earth color
18. a feud
19. a collection of documents about someone
20. to give support to (15)
22. having to do with heat
23. one who loads and unloads ships
24. a fixed, annual payment
25. a great number gathered together
28. failure to do what is required
29. a test of endurance
32. that cannot be undone or changed (15)
34. pretending to be high-minded or religious
37. that which remains
41. prefix meaning "new form of" (4)
43. a special fondness; a strong liking
46. a falling or dropping back
47. to declare positively; to assert
49. causing harm; destructive (15)
50. to do with the eyes or eyesight
51. warlike; unfriendly
52. to set free; to liberate
53. a distressing or awkward situation

DOWN

2. to throw overboard (to lighten a ship)
3. not stopping or slowing down
5. of or relating to great forces of nature
6. done or happening in an instant
7. having self-government
9. still existing
10. to oppose by argument; to disprove (7)
11. an excessive enthusiasm for something
12. a crude parody or mocking imitation of
13. farthest back; last
14. an authority on fine foods
16. an unrealistic play with good and evil
    greatly exaggerated
21. spirit; courage
26. to be a sign of; to announce
27. a right given by a company or by government
28. various; several
29. a written account; an autobiography
30. anger (5)
31. the highest point; the peak (3)
33. tormented; greatly worried or bothered
    (alternate spelling)
35. great wealth or richness
36. a swift and spirited horse
38. to declare blameless
39. happening from time to time; not regular
40. one who insists that things be done properly
42. greed for money
44. an ardent supporter or follower
45. refusing to give up; determined
48. all the plants of a region

74

Chapter Seven

Word List 19

ADHERENT	EPAULET	PEDAGOGUE
AMITY	GAMUT	PROSAIC
BLOATED	HYPOCHONDRIAC	REGALE
CATACLYSM	INTERIM	SUPERCILIOUS
DESICCATE	LUMINOUS	VITRIOLIC
DISHEVELED	MUNITIONS	

Look up the words above in your dictionary. Note that many of them have more than one meaning. When you think that you know *all* the meanings of *all* the words, go on to the exercise below.

EXERCISE 19A

From the four choices following each phrase or sentence, you are to circle the letter preceding the one that is closest in meaning to the italicized word. Where the same word appears more than once, you should note that it is being used in different senses.

1. a firm *adherent*
   (a) glue (b) supporter (c) principle (d) offer

2. lasting *amity*
   (a) bitterness (b) friendship (c) suspicion (d) contempt

3. a *bloated* face
   (a) angry (b) swollen (c) emaciated (d) bearded

4. a great *cataclysm*
   (a) period of history (b) mass movement of people (c) force of nature (d) sudden, violent change

5. to *desiccate* foods
   (a) chop up (b) destroy bacteria in (c) remove the water from (d) preserve by freezing

6. a *desiccated* personality
   (a) well-adjusted (b) drained of vitality (c) pleasant (d) well-known

7. a *disheveled* appearance
   (a) startled (b) rumpled (c) false (d) well-groomed

8. to adjust an *epaulet*
   (a) chain that supports a sword (b) tasseled shoulder decoration (c) leather strap that crosses over the shoulder (d) three-cornered hat

9. to run the *gamut*
   (a) entire range (b) gauntlet (c) naval blockade (d) racing circuit

10. to be a *hypochondriac*
    (a) person unduly worried over his or her health (b) person who is addicted to drugs (c) person with an unreasoning fear of heights (d) person who eats and drinks to excess

11. in the *interim*
    (a) inner room (b) intervening period (c) interconnecting passage (d) early stage

12. *luminous* heavenly bodies
    (a) invisible to the naked eye (b) giving off light (c) immensely distant (d) moving around the sun

13. a *luminous* piece of writing
    (a) obscure (b) terse (c) lengthy (d) clear

14. to produce *munitions*
    (a) farm equipment (b) processed foodstuffs (c) medical supplies (d) war supplies

15. an experienced *pedagogue*
    (a) political leader (b) schoolteacher (c) public speaker (d) children's doctor

16. a *prosaic* account
    (a) dull (b) exciting (c) poetic (d) obviously false

17. to *regale* them

(a) bore (b) entertain (c) distract (d) annoy

18. a *supercilious* person

(a) refined (b) haughty (c) important (d) delicate

19. a *vitriolic* attack

(a) large-scale (b) mild (c) vicious (d) unexpected

20. a bottle of *vitriol*

(a) lemon juice (b) distilled water (c) wine vinegar (d) sulphuric acid

Check your answers against the correct ones given below. The answers are not in order; this is to prevent your eye from catching sight of the correct answers before you have had a chance to do the exercise on your own.

16a. 4d. 10a. 14d. 7b. 11b. 18b. 6b. 2b. 12b. 5c. 1b. 19c. 15b. 9a. 17b. 8b. 13d. 3b. 20d.

Look up in your dictionary all the words for which you gave incorrect answers. Only when you have done this should you go on to the next exercise.

EXERCISE 19B

Each word in Word List 19 is used several times in the sentences below to illustrate different meanings or usage. One of the sentences for each word uses the italicized word incorrectly. You are to circle the letter preceding the sentence.

1. (a) The *adherent* wasn't strong enough to hold the broken parts together. (b) He is an *adherent* of the views of Charles Darwin. (c) This sect is noted for its *adherence* to the principles of the early church.

2. (a) Only where there is *amity* between nations can there be world peace. (b) A look of bitter *amity*, which she covered up with a forced smile, crossed her face. (c) There was bitter rivalry between the two groups although they kept up a pretense of *amity*.

3. The river, *bloated* by heavy rains, broke its banks. (b) From the *bloated* condition of the corpse, police believe it had been in the water for some time. (c) *Bloated* with pride, he told me for the hundredth time how he had won the contest. (d) I *bloated* all of the balloons for the children's Christmas party.

4. (a) The *cataclysm* is several hundred feet deep and extends for some twenty miles. (b) Everyone was swept up in the *cataclysm* of war. (c) A nuclear war would be a *cataclysmic* event. (d) The eruption of the Krakatoa volcano in 1883 was the worst *cataclysm* of its kind in modern times.

5. (a) The recipe calls for a cupful of *desiccated* coconut. (b) The four points on the diagram we will *desiccate* A, B, C, and D. (c) Forty years in that cramped, airless office had quite *desiccated* their personalities.

6. (a) She looked slightly *disheveled* when she emerged from under the car. (b) He borrowed a comb to arrange his *disheveled* locks. (c) The gravel had been *disheveled* right in the middle of the driveway.

7. (a) They were attired in full dress uniform, complete with gold tasseled *epaulets* on each shoulder. (b) After serving three months, cadets are promoted to the rank of *epaulet*. (c) Officers who are drummed out of their regiments have their *epaulets* torn from their shoulders.

8. (a) The plays in which she has appeared run the *gamut* from broad farce to Greek tragedy. (b) There was an almost *gamutless* choice before us. (c) His face registered the whole *gamut* of human emotions, from surprised joy to bitterest grief.

9. (a) The doctor gave me the injection with a long *hypochondriac* needle. (b) The great assortment of pills and medicines she carried with her were a good indication that she suffered from *hypochondria*. (c) The doctor's

waiting room was filled with *hypochondriacs* giving each other ideas for new ailments.

10. (a) He offered to *interim* the dispute but neither side was willing to talk. (b) This is an *interim* report, and it will be some months before the final report is ready. (c) In the *interim* between her arrival and departure, she told us a great deal about herself.

11. (a) *Luminous* paint glows in the dark. (b) These poems have a *luminous* quality that comes across even on a first reading. (c) The foliage was *luminous* with the bright sunlight filtering through the trees. (d) Lights from the boats in the harbor *luminoused* brightly in the water.

12. (a) *Munitions* workers were asked not to take vacations while the war was on. (b) The workers who produce *munitions* are as important as the soldiers who use them. (c) Despite our *munitions* to her not to leave, she did so the moment our backs were turned. (d) Enemy planes attacked a *munitions* factory in last night's raid.

13. (a) The *pedagogue* in him could not resist correcting the child's grammatical error. (b) She tried to *pedagogue* but found that teaching was not her forte. (c) The *pedagogues* who have charge of our children's education must be chosen with great care. (d) His field is *pedagogy*, and he writes frequently for educational journals.

14. (a) Inlaid in the floor was a colorful *prosaic* made of thousands of small tiles. (b) We lead very *prosaic* lives here in the country. (c) She can make the most *prosaic* piece of writing sound interesting.

15. (a) After a good dinner we *regaled* ourselves to our rooms for a much-needed sleep. (b) He *regaled* his guests with an account of his travels in Asia. (c) We *regaled* ourselves with the fine food and entertainment offered by the hotel. (d) The table, laden with steaming dishes of food, was a sight to *regale* the eye.

16. (a) Her *supercilious* attitude toward our efforts greatly annoyed us. (b) Anything that is *supercilious* to your needs should be returned. (c) His lip curled in a *supercilious* smile. (d) With a *supercilious* raising of her eyebrows, she expressed her utter contempt for us.

17. (a) A *vitriolic* solution will burn through metal. (b) Without any provocation, he launched a *vitriolic* attack upon my record while in office. (c) In a polite discussion there is no place for such *vitriolic* remarks. (d) She felt a sudden *vitriolic* pain between her shoulder blades.

EXERCISE 19C

Some of the italicized words in the sentences below are used literally; others are used metaphorically (these terms are explained in the Introduction). In the spaces provided write L if the word is used literally; if the word is used metaphorically, replace the metaphorical expression with a literal rendering. Be careful not to change the meaning of a sentence.

1. She *flew* ( ) to the door when she heard his knock.

2. The heavyweight champion is a *tiger* ( ) in the ring.

3. A fire was *burning* ( ) in the grate.

4. He had a *hand* ( ) in the project.

5. She was as ferocious as a *tiger* ( ).

6. *Cold* ( ) stares greeted him on his arrival.

7. Unemployment is one of the *burning* ( ) issues of the day.

8. A bird *flew* ( ) down and pecked at her.

9. He hurt his *hand* ( ) in the machine.

10. The room grew *cold* ( ), so I lit a fire.

WORDLY WISE 19

Note the spelling of DESICCATE; it has one *s* and two *c*'s.

A SUPERCILIOUS person may show his or her supposed superiority by a raising of the eyebrows; at any rate this is the literal meaning of the word. *Super* is the Latin for "above" and *cilium* is the Latin for "eyebrow."

Etymology

Study the roots and prefix given below, together with the English words derived from them. Capitalized words are those given in the Word List. You should look up in a dictionary any words that are unfamiliar to you.

Prefix: *ad-* (to) Latin — Examples: *ADHER-ENT, ad*jacent, *ad*join

Roots: *ped* (child) Greek — Examples: *PEDA-GOGUE, ped*iatrician

(Review) *here* (stick) Latin — Example: AD*HERE*NT

agein (to lead) Greek — Examples: PEDA*GOGUE*, dem*agogue*

Word List 20

AFFLUENT	EXODUS	OBLIVION
ASSUAGE	GENTEEL	PILLORY
BUTTE	INEBRIATED	PROVOCATION
COMPLACENT	INTROSPECTIVE	REVOKE
DESULTORY	MARTINET	TACIT
DISSERTATION		

Look up the words above in your dictionary. Note that many of them have more than one meaning. When you think that you know *all* the meanings of *all* words, go on to the exercise below.

EXERCISE 20A

From the four choices following each phrase or sentence, you are to circle the letter preceding the one that is closest in meaning to the italicized word. Where the same word appears more than once, you should note that it is being used in different senses.

1. an *affluent* person
   (a) sickly (b) wealthy (c) portly (d) hungry

2. to *assuage* someone's grief
   (a) cause (b) lessen (c) ignore (d) aggravate

3. We rode as far as the *butte*.
   (a) early Spanish-American church (b) steep cliff overlooking the sea (c) isolated, steep-sided hill (d) narrow, steep-sided valley

4. a *complacent* remark
   (a) self-satisfied (b) dissatisfied (c) complimentary (d) tolerant

5. *desultory* activities
   (a) aimless (b) frantic (c) methodical (d) secret

6. to complete a *dissertation*
   (a) journey to a holy shrine (b) thorough testing of a product (c) full cycle (d) formal essay

7. a mass *exodus*
   (a) protest (b) movement (c) departure (d) meeting

8. a *genteel* manner
   (a) boisterous (b) determined (c) mournful (d) polite and refined

9. an *inebriated* person
   (a) foolish (b) drunken (c) puzzled (d) forlorn

10. an *introspective* person
    (a) given to acting impulsively (b) given to examining one's own thoughts (c) given to moods of depression (d) given to violent mood changes

11. He is a *martinet*.
    (a) strict disciplinarian (b) veteran soldier (c) confused muddler (d) traveling priest

12. sweet *oblivion*
    (a) enchantment (b) charity (c) lack of awareness (d) revenge

13. punished by being locked in the *pillory*

(a) stool on the end of a beam that is lowered into a pond (b) wooden frame with holes for confining the head and hands (c) metal case that encloses and crushes the body (d) tiny, windowless prison cell

14. to give no *provocation*
    (a) cause for anger (b) mercy (c) sign of alarm (d) reason

15. to *revoke* a license
    (a) issue (b) withdraw (c) renew (d) extend

16. a *tacit* agreement
    (a) written (b) verbal (c) unspoken (d) secret

Check your answers against the correct ones given below. The answers are not in order; this is to prevent your eye from catching sight of the correct answers before you have had a chance to do the exercise on your own.

6d. 11a. 9b. 15b. 4a. 14a. 1b. 5a. 2b. 7c. 13b. 10b. 8d. 12c. 16c. 3c.

Look up in your dictionary all the words for which you gave incorrect answers. Only when you have done this should you go on to the next exercise.

EXERCISE 20B

Each word in Word List 20 is used several times in the sentences below to illustrate different meanings or usage. One of the sentences for each word uses the italicized word incorrectly. You are to circle the letter preceding the sentence.

1. (a) The United States, with its great abundance of material wealth, has been called "the *affluent* society." (b) She is *affluent* in five languages. (c) The discovery of oil on their land brought them sudden *affluence*. (d) She invested her money wisely when she was young and now lives in *affluent* circumstances.

2. (a) We *assuaged* our hands and faces in a little mountain stream. (b) He set aside his own sorrow in an attempt to *assuage* hers. (c) Nothing could *assuage* her grief on receiving the tragic news. (d) We had had more than enough food to *assuage* our hunger.

3. (a) He nestled the *butte* of the rifle against his cheek and took careful aim. (b) From the top of the *butte* we could see in all directions. (c) The town of *Butte*, Montana, gets its name from the nearby rock formation.

4. (a) We must not become *complacent* just because we have won three games in a row. (b) Getting fired from his job severely jolted his *complacency*. (c) The judge ordered that the *complacent* in the case be awarded damages. (d) The report's findings that our defense system is inadequate ought to reduce the *complacency* of those in government.

5. (a) It was such a *desultory* day that we just sat lazily around and did nothing. (b) The children picked *desultorily* at their food. (c) Talk was *desultory* as we sat around killing time. (d) She attended classes in *desultory* fashion for two months before dropping out of school.

6. (a) She was engaged in a long *dissertation* with the cook in which both were in danger of losing their tempers. (b) Upon the completion of her *dissertation* she will receive her M.A. degree. (c) His *dissertation* was entitled "Economic Effects of Boll Weevil Control in the Mississippi Delta Region."

7. (a) The *exodus* of the middle class to the suburbs shows no sign of stopping. (b) She leaves for London shortly, but the date of her *exodus* has not yet been fixed. (c) A sudden scream of "Fire!" caused a panic-stricken *exodus* from the theater. (d) The second book of the Bible tells of the *exodus* of the Israelites from Egypt.

8. (a) "I don't allow coarse language in my house," he said *genteelly*. (b) His *genteel* manner could instantly be set aside when it

came time to strike a bargain. (c) She had tried to *genteel* her two sons to act like gentlemen. (d) His *genteel* background did not fit him for frontier life.

9. (a) A number of power line poles were *inebriated* in last night's storm. (b) He had had several drinks too many and was quite *inebriated*. (c) *Inebriated* with excitement at our success, we hurled our caps into the air.

10. (a) The museum is holding an *introspective* exhibition of Jackson Pollock's paintings. (b) Keeping a diary has made her *introspective*. (c) Early psychologists practiced *introspection*; they studied themselves.

11. (a) The *martinet* is a small, swallow-like bird with a forked tail and blue-black head. (b) The new boss must be a real *martinet*, for she maintains strict discipline at all times.

12. (a) The spearheads are made out of *oblivion* or similar hard material. (b) He stared ahead in a trance, *oblivious* to his surroundings. (c) The publisher has rescued the author from *oblivion* by bringing out a new edition of her works. (d) Overcome with weariness, the runner fell onto the bed and sank into *oblivion*.

13. (a) The governor was *pilloried* in the newspapers for her refusal to take a firm stand. (b) Petty offenders were placed in the *pillory*, where they were targets for the abuse and the rotten vegetables of their neighbors. (c) The newspapers have launched a violent *pillory* against the mayor. (d) A man or woman guilty of a minor offense would be *pilloried* for a few hours and then released.

14. (a) The president issued a *provocation* declaring June 14 National Hot Dog Day. (b) The gangs of youths in the city would attack each other on the slightest *provocation*. (c) His dumping garbage on my front lawn was a deliberately *provocative* act. (d) Don't let them *provoke* you into losing your temper.

15. (a) They *revoked* her bitterly for her refusal to help. (b) His authority to appoint minor officials can be *revoked* if he misuses it. (c) A doctor found guilty of improper practices may have her license *revoked*. (d) This license is issued subject to immediate *revocation* if it is used improperly.

16. (a) I looked at her, and she nodded in *tacit* agreement. (b) She smiled, *tacitly* assuring him that he was welcome. (c) There was a *tacit* understanding between them that each would help the other if needed. (d) He was a slow-moving, *tacit* man, as they all are in those parts.

EXERCISE 20C

From the five numbered choices, complete the analogies below by underlining the word that stands in the same relationship to the third word as the second word does to the first. An explanation of analogies is given in the Introduction.

1. scalp:skin :: cranium: (1) skull (2) head (3) skeleton (4) hair (5) bone

2. warlike:peaceful :: belligerent: (1) angry (2) enemy (3) pacific (4) country (5) retaliate

3. homogeneous:heterogeneous :: uniform: (1) soldier (2) army (3) few (4) mixed (5) many

4. aqueous:water :: thermal: (1) ice (2) heat (3) solid (4) cool (5) warm

5. fauna:animal :: flora: (1) vegetable (2) flower (3) stem (4) leaf (5) plant

6. verbal:spoken :: tacit: (1) word (2) written (3) speech (4) heard (5) unspoken

7. oral:mouth :: ocular: (1) eye (2) nose (3) throat (4) teeth (5) ear

8. metal:mettle :: scene: (1) view (2) seen (3) screen (4) play (5) picture

9. highwayman:stagecoaches :: freebooter:
(1) seas (2) ships (3) treasure (4) pirates
(5) booty

10. gluttony:food :: avarice: (1) drink
(2) greedy (3) hungry (4) money (5) poverty

WORDLY WISE 20

A BUTTE (pronounced *byoot*) is an isolated, steep-sided hill. A *butt* (pronounced *but*) may be (1) the thick end of something (a rifle *butt*), (2) the end left over (a cigar *butt*), (3) a large wine barrel, (4) the object of teasing or ridicule (He was the *butt* of all their jokes). *Butt* is also a verb and means "to strike or bump with the head" (goats *butt*).

Note the different spellings of COMPLACENT and *complaisant*; these two words are homonyms and are discussed in Lesson 13.

A PILLORY was a wooden frame in which a person's head, and sometimes also his or her hands, were locked. Thus imprisoned, he or she was the target for the abuse and missiles of the people of the town. The verb *pillory*, meaning "to scorn publicly," comes from the use of this machine. A similar means of punishment was the *stocks*; in this the prisoner's feet, sometimes also his or her hands, were locked, and he or she received the same treatment. Both pillory and stocks passed out of use some 150 years ago.

Etymology

Study the roots and prefixes given below, together with the English words derived from them. Capitalized words are those given in the Word List. You should look up in a dictionary any words that are unfamiliar to you.

Prefixes: *pro-* (forth) Latin — Examples: *PROVOCATION*, *pro*test, *pro*spect
(Review) *re-* (back) Latin — Example: *RE*VOKE
(Review) *intro-* (into) Latin — Example: *INTRO*SPECTIVE

Roots: *voca* (call) Latin — Examples: PRO*VO*CATION, RE*VOKE*
spect (look) Latin — Examples: INTRO*SPECT*IVE, *spect*acles, pro*spect*

Word List 21

ALLOY	FINITE	OBSOLESCENT
AUGURY	GUILLOTINE	PREFATORY
CADAVER	INEVITABLE	RECLUSE
DECRY	IRREFUTABLE	SOMNAMBULIST
DEVISE	MILITANT	TELEPATHY
ENTREAT		

Look up the words above in your dictionary. Note that many of them have more than one meaning. When you think that you know *all* the meanings of *all* the words, go on to the exercise below.

EXERCISE 21A

From the four choices following each phrase or sentence, you are to circle the letter preceding the one that is closest in meaning to the italicized word. Where the same word appears more than once, you should note that it is being used in different senses.

1. a light *alloy*
(a) metal boat (b) two-wheeled carriage (c) mixture of gases (d) mixture of metals

2. an *augury* of the future
(a) fear (b) omen (c) vision (d) account

3. to examine the *cadaver*
(a) set of reasons (b) body of evidence (c) dead body (d) stated proposition

4. to *decry* such behavior
(a) denounce (b) encourage (c) ignore (d) observe

5. to *devise* a plan
(a) stick to (b) change (c) suggest (d) work out

6. to *entreat* someone
(a) guard (b) beg (c) promise (d) accompany

7. a *finite* number
(a) large (b) limited (c) small (d) unlimited

8. sent to the *guillotine*

(a) high court of a country (b) machine for beheading people (c) upper chamber of a legislative body (d) remotest region of a country

9. to be *inevitable*

(a) unnecessary (b) unavoidable (c) undeniable (d) uncertain

10. an *irrefutable* argument

(a) that goes around in a circle (b) that cannot be disputed (c) that is repeated over and over (d) that is expressed in its simplest form

11. a *militant* group

(a) well-disciplined (b) aggressively active (c) army, navy, or air force (d) enemy

12. to be *obsolescent*

(a) outdated but still usable (b) useless because outdated (c) quite up to date (d) still in the planning stage

13. *prefatory* remarks

(a) introductory (b) flattering (c) insulting (d) concluding

14. to be a *recluse*

(a) boor (b) hermit (c) genius (d) madman

15. to be a *somnambulist*

(a) musician (b) secret agent (c) circus performer (d) sleepwalker

16. experiments in *telepathy*

(a) underwater travel (b) thought transference (c) space travel (d) mind expanding

Check your answers against the correct ones given below. The answers are not in order; this is to prevent your eye from catching sight of the correct answers before you have had a chance to do the exercise on your own.

8b. 12a. 16b. 3c. 2b. 7b. 13a. 10b. 14b. 1d. 5d. 6b. 11b. 9b. 15d. 4a.

Look up in your dictionary all the words for which you gave incorrect answers. Only when you have done this should you go on to the next exercise.

EXERCISE 21B

Each word in Word List 21 is used several times in the sentences below to illustrate different meanings or usage. One of the sentences for each word uses the *italicized* word incorrectly. You are to circle the letter preceding the sentence.

1. (a) Brass is an *alloy* of copper and zinc. (b) We *alloyed* their fears by pointing out that the noise they had heard was only the wind. (c) An *alloy* possesses properties that are quite different from each of its component metals. (d) With pure and *unalloyed* joy we welcomed them into our midst.

2. (a) Their great enthusiasm is a certain *augury* of their future success. (b) Her refusal to accept the post was, in my opinion, a very *augury* decision. (c) He believed the cat that crossed his path to be an *augury* of his own good fortune. (d) The fact that she has been fired from her last five jobs does not *augur* well for her future.

3. (a) The teacher came over to see what all the *cadaver* was about. (b) Medical students learn anatomy by dissecting *cadavers*. (c) The dim, green lighting gave his face a *cadaverous* pallor.

4. (a) In favoring pure research, I am not in any way *decrying* applied research. (b) It is not enough to *decry* air pollution; one must do something about it. (c) We ignored their *decries* that they had been cheated out of their money.

5. (a) A turbine is a *devise* for converting water power into electrical energy. (b) This is an operation of my own *devising*. (c) I have *devised* a training program that will shortly be put into effect.

6. (a) I *entreat* you to take care of my little

brother. (b) We ignored their *entreaties* as we thought that we knew what was best. (c) "Please stay a little longer," she said *entreatingly*. (d) They grew *entreatingly* worried as months passed with no word from their children.

7. (a) Is the universe *finite*, or does it have no boundaries? (b) The human mind, being *finite*, cannot wholly grasp the idea of God. (c) This is a useful tool, but it is somewhat *finite* in what it can do. (d) Although it would be astronomically large, the number of grains of sand in the world could be expressed as a *finite* number.

8. (a) Louis XVI and Marie Antoinette of France were *guillotined* in 1792. (b) With a mighty swing of his sword, he *guillotined* the head of his opponent. (c) Until 1981, the *guillotine* was the method of execution in France.

9. (a) A certain loss of liquid through evaporation is *inevitable*. (b) If our nation's just demands are not met, war will be *inevitable*. (c) With *inevitable* aim she shot three arrows into the center of the target. (d) Loss of hair and gaining weight are the *inevitable* consequences of middle age, some believe.

10. (a) He's such an *irrefutable* person that I don't have the heart to refuse him. (b) She was able to demonstrate *irrefutably* that she had not written the article. (c) It is useless to argue, as the facts in the case are *irrefutable*.

11. (a) Labor unions are *militantly* opposed to laws limiting their right to strike. (b) They are *militant* civil rights workers. (c) Do not do anything that might *militant* against your being chosen. (d) She had been a *militant* in the votes-for-women movement.

12. (a) Give the names of any students who are *obsolescent* to the principal's secretary. (b) Because of the need for constant and rapid development, modern weapons quickly become *obsolescent*. (c) Items that are *obsolescent* are sold to foreign countries, but obsolete items are scrapped. (d) Planned *obsolescence* is the deliberate making of consumer goods in such a way that they quickly need replacing.

13. (a) They insisted that they did not want their children to receive *prefatory* treatment. (b) The chairperson made a few *prefatory* remarks before calling on the first speaker.

14. (a) After the death of her friend, she became a *recluse* and shut herself away in that big house. (b) He became very *reclusive* and refused to answer any questions. (c) He became very *reclusive* as he grew older and seldom emerged from his room.

15. (a) She joined a team of *somnambulists* in a circus when she was twelve years old. (b) A *somnambulist* should be led quietly back to bed without being awakened. (c) People in a state of *somnambulism* seldom hurt themselves during their nighttime wanderings.

16. (a) Experiments in *telepathy* have yet to prove conclusively that thoughts can be transferred. (b) The two brothers claim to be able to communicate *telepathically*, even when several miles apart. (c) By means of radio *telepathy* messages can be flashed instantly to every part of the globe.

EXERCISE 21C

This exercise combines synonyms and antonyms. You are to underline the word which is *either* most similar in meaning *or* most nearly opposite in meaning to the CAPITALIZED word. Underline only one word for each question after deciding that it is *either* an antonym *or* a synonym, and write A (for antonym) or S (for synonym) after the capitalized word. Allow only fifteen minutes for this test. If you cannot answer a question, go on to the next one without delay. If you have time left over at the end, go back and try to fill in unanswered questions.

1. INNOCENT .....
militant culpable obsolescent tacit complacent

2. BLESSING .....
benison pillory provocation oblivion gourmet

3. CORPSE .....
ocular bloated guillotine cadaver residue

4. IMPROVE .....
devise retrogress recluse sojourn franchise

5. GRANT .....
revoke alloy emancipate extant herald

6. HARMLESS .....
sanctimonious prefatory pernicious bombastic prosaic

7. WEALTHY .....
bestial supercilious impeccable affluent sanctimonious

8. PEACEFUL .....
hypochondriac pacific recluse luminous unremitting

9. EXTOL .....
regale prate decry survey demote

10. DISSATISFIED .....
addled supercilious congenital complacent salutary

11. WILLING .....
chary taciturn palliative redoubtable replete

12. SLEEPWALKER .....
pedagogue adherent stickler censer somnambulist

13. INBORN .....
insidious belligerent hindmost inclement congenital

14. DEPARTURE .....
vendetta partiality exodus travesty transition

15. OMEN .....
dossier augury gamut vendetta thrall

16. ASSERT .....
affirm ogle demote harangue demoralize

17. COARSE .....
prosaic luminous genteel spectral filial

18. CLUMSY .....
disheveled bloated maladroit vitriolic indignity

19. HERMIT .....
recluse predicament courser forte mendicant

20. POVERTY .....
chattel travesty ennui chaste penury

21. SOBER .....
belligerent inebriated disheveled parsimonious complacent

22. BRIEF .....
pacific pernicious parsimonious marathon desultory

23. BEG .....
endorse regale entreat surfeit assuage

24. BEGGAR .....
chattel canker arbiter mendicant recluse

25. FORGETFULNESS .....
oblivion avarice propaganda inferno augury

26. UNSPOKEN .....
chary tacit sporadic autonomous somnambulist

27. TINY . . . . .
    autonomous amity mercenary symmetrical prodigious

28. DISCIPLINARIAN . . . . .
    scrip hypochondriac pedagogue chattel martinet

29. UNBOUNDED . . . . .
    vitriolic adherent verbatim finite incognito

30. SPARKLE . . . . .
    exonerate bauble prate bizarre scintillate

WORDLY WISE 21

In ancient Rome, the citizens, even the government, based many decisions on omens thought to show the will of Jupiter. If signs were unfavorable, the Senate postponed its meetings; the army did not set out for war. Of particular importance were thunder, lightning, falling stars, and the behavior of such birds as the eagle, owl, or raven. Rome's official interpreters of these omens were the *augurs*, and from this practice comes our word AUGURY, designating the art of telling the future from signs; an omen or sign; or any indication of things to come. *Augur* (or *auguere*) means "sooth-sayer," and *to augur* means to predict the future by interpreting signs, or "to presage or portend."

Do not confuse this word with *auger*, a homonym of *augur*. An *auger* is a tool used for drilling.

Distinguish between DECRY (to express strong disapproval of) and *descry* (catch sight of; to find out; to discover).

DEVISE (pronounced *di-VYZ* or *dee-VYZ*) is a verb and means "to work out" or "to think up." *Device* (pronounced *di-VYS* or *dee-VYS)* is a noun and means "something made for a particular purpose." (I was able to *devise* a *device* that will do the job.)

OBSOLESCENT means "outdated but still usable." *Obsolete* means "no longer of use because outdated."

Etymology

Study the roots and prefix given below, together with the English words derived from them. Capitalized words are those given in the Word List. You should look up in a dictionary any words that are unfamiliar to you.

Prefix: *de-* (down) Latin — Examples: *DECRY, de*cline, *de*scend

Roots: *tele* (distance) Greek — Examples: *TELE*PATHY, *tele*scope, *tele*phone

patho (feeling) Greek — Examples: TELE*PATHY, patho*s, sym*pathy*

ACROSS

1. to lessen (pain, grief, hunger)
4. a sign foretelling future events
7. viciously sharp and biting; caustic
12. one unduly worried over his or her health
14. to work out; to contrive
15. one who lives alone; a hermit
17. to withdraw or cancel
18. transference of thoughts between persons
20. under the influence of alcohol
24. dull; commonplace
25. certain to happen; unavoidable
27. to scorn publicly
28. a long formal essay or discourse
31. one who maintains strict discipline
32. an entire range from one extreme to the other
34. cause for anger or retaliation
39. overly refined, polite, or well-bred
40. that cannot be disputed
42. to remove the water from; to dry out
43. to ask earnestly; to beg
44. a shoulder ornament on military uniforms
45. friendly, peaceful relations
46. swollen, as with water or air
47. outdated but still usable
48. in loose disorder; rumpled
49. coming at the beginning; introductory

DOWN

1. a supporter or follower
2. proud and scornful; haughty
3. a mass departure
4. rotten, said of eggs (10)
5. a machine for beheading people
6. a turning for help or assistance (4)
8. being a natural part of someone or something (4)
9. the period intervening; meantime
10. giving off light; glowing
11. a corpse, especially one used for dissecting
13. lacking purpose; aimless
16. self-satisfied; smug
19. not expressed openly but implied; unspoken
21. an isolated, steep-sided hill
22. a mixture of two or more metals
23. aggressively active; ready to fight
24. a schoolmaster; a teacher
25. looking into one's own thoughts
26. a sleepwalker
29. a sudden, violent change; an upheaval
30. having limits; bounded
33. weapons and ammunition; war supplies
35. the state of being forgotten; forgetfulness
36. to entertain; to give pleasure to
37. greatly abundant; wealthy
38. to express strong disapproval of
41. filled; plentifully supplied (12)

Chapter Eight

Word List 22

AMENABLE	EXTINCT	PACIFY
AUTOMATON	FIASCO	PEJORATIVE
CEDE	GIRD	PRACTICABLE
DECIDUOUS	INCEPTION	PUNITIVE
DISCREDIT	LIMBO	SOMATIC
DISPARAGE		

Look up the words above in your dictionary. Note that many of them have more than one meaning. When you think that you know *all* the meanings of *all* the words, go on to the exercise below.

EXERCISE 22A

From the four choices following each phrase or sentence, you are to circle the letter preceding the one that is closest in meaning to the italicized word. Where the same word appears more than once, you should note that it is being used in different senses.

1. *amenable* to discipline
   (a) harmful (b) oblivious (c) immune (d) responsive

2. an ingenious *automaton*
   (a) designer of machines (b) perpetual motion machine (c) self-regulating machine (d) piece of sculpture with moving parts

3. to *cede* the property
   (a) develop (b) surrender (c) measure (d) recover

4. a *deciduous* tree
   (a) that sheds its leaves (b) evergreen (c) that produces fruit (d) tropical

5. to *discredit* their story
   (a) have an open mind concerning (b) throw doubt on (c) demand proof of (d) accept

6. to *disparage* her achievement
   (a) belittle (b) envy (c) admire (d) emulate

7. the species is *extinct*
   (a) of very great age (b) still existing (c) in danger of dying out (d) no longer in existence

8. It was a *fiasco*!
   (a) gay, lively party (b) place for sleeping (c) ridiculous failure (d) open courtyard

9. *girded* by trees
   (a) sparsely covered (b) encircled (c) crisscrossed (d) thickly covered

10. he *girded* on his sword
    (a) raised in salute (b) fastened with a belt (c) raised in battle (d) replaced in its scabbard

11. the plan's *inception*
    (a) beginning (b) end (c) development (d) purpose

12. in *limbo*
    (a) a condition of slavery (b) a condition of oblivion (c) a condition of disgrace (d) a condition of helplessness

13. to *pacify* him
    (a) soothe (b) anger (c) ignore (d) tolerate

14. to *pacify* a country
    (a) conquer (b) invade (c) bring peace to (d) divide by civil war

15. *pejorative* terms
    (a) that are accurately descriptive (b) that tend to give an unfavorable impression (c) that tend to give a favorable impression (d) that are vague and imprecise

16. to be *practicable*
    (a) worn out after heavy use (b) still in the experimental stage (c) capable of being put into use (d) highly experienced

17. *punitive* measures

(a) punishing (b) puny (c) prompt (d) precise

18. *somatic* diseases

(a) chronic (b) mental (c) minor (d) bodily

Check your answers against the correct ones given below. The answers are not in order; this is to prevent your eye from catching sight of the correct answers before you have had a chance to do the exercise on your own.

6a. 2c. 8c. 12b. 18d. 14c. 11a. 9b. 1d. 7d. 16c. 13a. 5b. 15b. 4a. 17a. 10b. 3b.

Look up in your dictionary all the words for which you gave incorrect answers. Only when you have done this should you go on to the next exercise.

EXERCISE 22B

Each word in Word List 22 is used several times in the sentences below to illustrate different meanings or usage. One of the sentences for each word uses the italicized word incorrectly. You are to circle the letter preceding the sentence.

1. (a) The town is fairly remote, but it has all the *amenables* of civilization. (b) He was *amenable* to our suggestion that we begin at once. (c) Since the child is not *amenable* to strict discipline, we decided to try kindness.

2. (a) In the homes of the future all household chores will be performed by *automatons*. (b) He moved like an *automaton*, his steps stiff and unnatural. (c) *Automaton* is a system of manufacture in which all operations are performed and regulated by machines.

3. (a) Spain *ceded* Puerto Rico to the United States in 1898. (b) I regret that I cannot *cede* to your request. (c) She *ceded* the land to the state after providing for its development as a park.

4. (a) He hates having to do anything as *decidu-* *ous* as making up his mind. (b) Most of the trees are *deciduous*, so we are kept busy raking up the leaves every fall. (c) Elm, oak, and maple trees are *deciduous*; holly, spruce, and cedar trees are evergreen.

5. (a) Their shocking behavior has *discredited* them in the eyes of their associates. (b) The money has been *discredited* and transferred to your account. (c) It is much to your *discredit* that you refused to stay and accept the responsibility. (d) He has a tendency to lie, which *discredits* anything he might say on the subject.

6. (a) We must stop *disparaging* their efforts and try to help them. (b) I ignored their *disparaging* remarks as I knew they were jealous. (c) Try not to be *disparaged* by your failure; make up your mind to try harder next time. (d) My remarks were intended to be helpful and were not a *disparagement* of your efforts.

7. (a) Dinosaurs became *extinct* millions of years ago. (b) The region has many *extinct* volcanoes as well as one or two that are still active. (c) She collapsed suddenly on the street and was *extinct* when they got her to the hospital. (d) The whooping crane faces *extinction* unless efforts are made to preserve the species.

8. (a) I felt a complete *fiasco* when I found myself unable to remember a single word of my speech. (b) The meeting was a *fiasco* as none of the speakers turned up. (c) Our demonstration of our unsinkable boat turned into a *fiasco* when it overturned and sank.

9. (a) With a mighty leap the horse *girded* the river. (b) They *girded* on their swords and sounded the call to battle. (c) A purple sash was *girded* about her waist. (d) We must *gird* ourselves for a prolonged and bitter struggle.

10. (a) I have had grave doubts about this project since the day of its *inception*. (b) You can have no *inception* of the difficulty of the task we have set ourselves.

11. (a) She walked around before the start of the race to *limbo* up her muscles. (b) Some Christians believed that the souls of unbaptized infants spent some time in *Limbo* before being admitted to heaven. (c) He has gone to that special *limbo* reserved for defeated politicians. (d) They existed uncertainly in that *limbo* of those who wait without any expectation of being attended to.

12. (a) Rebel bands still roamed the area, so marines were sent in to *pacify* the country. (b) Whenever the baby cried, the parents stuck a *pacify* in its mouth. (c) We *pacified* the baby by giving it some beads to play with. (d) Seeing his rage mounting by the minute, we did what we could to *pacify* him.

13. (a) "Abnormal" is a *pejorative* term, and psychiatrists prefer the more neutral "para-normal." (b) If you're still feeling *pejorative* tomorrow, go to see your doctor. (c) The word "pedagogue" is *pejorative* because it connotes excessive formality and rigidity.

14. (a) If the finance committee decides that the plan is *practicable*, it will put up the money. (b) They are *practicable* people with no use for theories.

15. (a) Such *punitive* laws ought to be replaced by others that are more humane. (b) A *punitive* expedition was launched against the rebellious region. (c) They received two thousand dollars in *punitive* damages and five hundred dollars in compensation for the libel against them. (d) The car undergoes extremely *punitive* tests to ensure its ruggedness.

16. (a) I have been feeling *somatic* and am confined to my bed. (b) Doctors feel that many mental disorders have *somatic* origins.

EXERCISE 22C

From the Latin word *poena* we derive the root *pena* (also written *puni* or *peni*). Complete the words below for which prefixes and suffixes have been supplied by filling in the appropriate form of this root. Give a brief definition of each word in the space provided. Basing your answer on an understanding of the common idea underlying each of the words below, write out what you think the Latin word *poena* means.

1. _____ L

....

2. _____ TENT

....

3. _____ SH

....

4. _____ TENTIARY

....

5. IM _____ TY

....

6. _____ TIVE

....

7. _____ NCE

....

8. _____ LTY

....

9. _____ LIZE

....

10. *poena* means

....

WORDLY WISE 22

In the teachings of the Catholic church,

LIMBO was the abode of the souls of children who died without receiving baptism into the church. Also in this place were the souls of all who had died without being made aware of the possibility of salvation through Christ. In this meaning the word is spelled with a capital *l*, *Limbo*. Because such souls were believed to be neither in heaven nor in hell, the term *limbo* has come to mean any place or condition in which one is forgotten or neglected.

PRACTICABLE means "capable of being put into practice"; *practical* means "sensible, realistic." A person may be *practical* but not *practicable;* however, a particular project may be both *practical* (sensible) and *practicable* (capable of being put into practice). A person may decide on a *practical* course of action that becomes no longer *practicable* because of changed conditions.

Word List 23

APOLOGIST	EXTREMIST	PALPITATE
BIANNUAL	EXTROVERT	PERPETRATE
CHRONOMETER	FLORID	PRESENTIMENT
DEFINITIVE	GIST	REQUITE
DISCREET	INTIMATE	STALACTITE
ENUNCIATE	LOPE	

Look up the words above in your dictionary. Note that many of them have more than one meaning. When you think that you know *all* the meanings of *all* the words, go on to the exercise below.

EXERCISE 23A

From the four choices following each phrase or sentence, you are to circle the letter preceding the one that is closest in meaning to the italicized word. Where the same word appears more than once, you should note that it is being used in different senses.

1. an active *apologist*
   (a) attacker of a policy or action (b) defender of a policy or action (c) plotter against a lawful government (d) defender of those charged with crimes

2. a *biannual* event
   (a) every two years (b) twice a year (c) every four years (d) four times a year

3. to adjust the *chronometer*
   (a) device for measuring distance (b) extremely accurate timepiece (c) device for beating musical time (d) device for measuring engine speeds

4. a *definitive* version
   (a) final (b) tentative (c) clear (d) partial

5. a *discreet* manner
   (a) offensively secretive (b) cautiously tactful (c) somewhat questionable (d) honestly straightforward

6. to *enunciate* the words
   (a) write out (b) make up (c) love the sound of (d) speak clearly

7. to *enunciate* a theory
   (a) investigate (b) denounce (c) set forth (d) defend

8. an *extremist*
   (a) person who holds immoderate views (b) person who sees all sides of a question (c) person who can trace his or her family through many generations (d) person who believes in many gods

9. an *extrovert*
   (a) person who dwells on the future (b) person who dwells on the past (c) person whose thoughts are directed inward (d) person whose thoughts are directed outward

10. a *florid* face
    (a) red (b) pale (c) puffy (d) drawn

11. the *gist* of the story
    (a) title (b) plot development (c) main point (d) moral

12. to *intimate* something
    (a) deliver (b) hide (c) suggest (d) reveal

13. an *intimate* theatre
    (a) small (b) private (c) public (d) out of the way

14. an *intimate* knowledge

(a) superficial (b) thorough (c) dangerous
(d) shared

15. *intimate* thoughts

(a) freely shared (b) vague (c) deeply private
(d) clearly expressed

16. to *lope* along

(a) move jerkily (b) move easily (c) slink
guiltily (d) inch slowly

17. to begin to *palpitate*

(a) beat rapidly (b) slow down (c) enlarge
(d) shrink

18. to *perpetrate* a crime

(a) be guilty of (b) admit (c) cover up
(d) solve

19. to have a *presentiment*

(a) feeling of impending misfortune (b) violent reaction to something said or done
(c) strong attachment to a person or place
(d) gift for foretelling the future

20. to *requite* a favor

(a) ask for (b) repay (c) ignore (d) resent

21. to *requite* his love

(a) reject (b) return (c) demand (d) need

22. a large *stalactite*

(a) a country that is totally dependent on
another (b) prisoner of war camp (c) artificial
body circling the earth (d) hanging, iciclelike
formation

Check your answers against the correct ones
given below. The answers are not in order; this is to
prevent your eye from catching sight of the correct
answers before you have had a chance to do the
exercise on your own.

6d. 13a. 11c. 18a. 7c. 17a. 1b. 15c. 22d. 10a. 14b.
9d. 21b. 4a. 2b. 12c. 19a. 5b. 16b. 20b. 3b. 8a.

Look up in your dictionary all the words for
which you gave incorrect answers. Only when you
have done this should you go on to the next
exercise.

EXERCISE 23B

Each word in Word List 23 is used several
times in the sentences below to illustrate different
meanings or usage. One of the sentences for each
word uses the italicized word incorrectly. You are
to circle the letter preceding the sentence.

1. (a) She was an *apologist* for a number of
discredited causes in the 1930s. (b) He was
extremely *apologist* for the trouble he had
caused.

2. (a) The club holds its *biannual* exhibitions in
March and October. (b) Marigolds and other
biannuals live for only one season. (c) Because
of their success, we will be holding concerts
biannually instead of once a year.

3. (a) The winning car was one tenth of a
chronometer ahead of the second-place car.
(b) When an ordinary watch is not accurate
enough, a *chronometer* is used.

4. (a) They seemed very *definitive* about not
wanting to go. (b) We now have *definitive*
proof that life does not exist on Venus. (c) The
present biography is satisfactory, but the
definitive work on this scientist's life has not
yet been written.

5. (a) He drew me aside and *discreetly* warned
me to be careful of what I said. (b) A gas
consists of *discreet* molecules loosely held
together. (c) A few *discreet* inquiries revealed
that the woman we were seeking was in the
district. (d) It was rather *indiscreet* of her to
tell them where we were going.

6. (a) Einstein *enunciated* his theory of relativity
in 1905. (b) He was *enunciated* as a traitor to
his country. (c) Our French teacher makes us
enunciate every word when we read aloud.
(d) A clear *enunciation* of our aims in Asia is
badly needed.

7. (a) Politicians who hold middle-of-the-road views are attacked by *extremists* of both the right and the left wing. (b) Only in the most *extremist* circumstances may the governor call out the National Guard. (c) She belongs to an *extremist* group that is plotting the overthrow of the government.

8. (a) You managed to *extrovert* yourself from what could have been a difficult situation. (b) *Extroverts* tend to be interested in other people and make good salespeople. (c) He is one of those *extroverted* people who are the life of the party.

9. (a) She took out a handful of coins and selected a *florid* which she gave to the man. (b) He had the *florid* countenance of a man who consumes large amounts of alcohol. (c) The *florid* style of nineteenth-century art makes it seem hopelessly outdated today.

10. (a) Just give me the *gist* of what she said. (b) The wheat is threshed to separate the *gist* from the chaff.

11. (a) She has an *intimate* grasp of the problem. (b) They *intimated* that they would try to help me. (c) In the more *intimate* surroundings of the club she became quite talkative. (d) This country will not be *intimated* by violence or the threat of violence.

12. (a) From the effortless way she *loped* around the track, it was easy to see she was going to win. (b) He tripped and fell in an undignified *lope* at our feet. (c) The wolf can keep up a steady *lope* for hours at a time.

13. (a) The sudden shock made her heart *palpitate*. (b) They *palpitated* the fruit with a fork before feeding it to the baby. (c) Violent exercise causes *palpitation* of the heart.

14. (a) Who could have *perpetrated* such a wicked deed? (b) He *perpetrated* his name by having a park named after himself. (c) They *perpetrated* a number of ingenious frauds for which they were never brought to book. (d) We refused to allow them to *perpetrate* any more of their terrible jokes.

15. (a) When the tide came in unexpectedly, we found ourselves in quite a *presentiment*. (b) He had a sudden *presentiment* that someone was lurking behind the door. (c) It is natural to have *presentiments* of misfortune, but this is due simply to nervousness.

16. (a) The pangs of *unrequited* love are the most painful of all. (b) She borrowed a hundred dollars which she promised to *requite* in twelve monthly payments. (c) We will never rest until you have been *requited* for your kindness.

17. (a) Poland and East Germany are *stalactites* of Russia. (b) *Stalactites* grow downward from the roofs of caves, while stalagmites grow upward from the floor. (c) As the water droplets evaporate from the roofs of caves, limestone, which gradually forms *stalactites*, is left. (d) A *stalactite* may grow only a few inches in a hundred years.

EXERCISE 23C

In each of the sentences below a word is omitted. From the four words provided, select the one that best completes the sentence. Allow ten minutes for this test. If you cannot answer a question, go on to the next one without delay. If you have time left over at the end, go back and try to fill in unanswered questions.

18 or over correct:	excellent
14 to 17 correct:	good
13 or under correct:	thorough review of A exercises indicated

1. Long .... hung from the roof of the cave.
   apologists stalactites fiascos auguries

2. Her face registered the whole .... of human emotions.
   amity interim gamut exodus

3. I had a . . . . that some misfortune was about to befall us.
presentiment provocation pejorative dissertation

4. The thief was locked securely in the . . . .
martinet chronometer stalactite pillory

5. Guns, planes, tanks, and other . . . . are needed to win the war.
munitions militants pejoratives automatons

6. The object gave off a . . . . glow.
tacit genteel prosaic luminous

7. She . . . . the audience with an account of her travels in Africa.
desiccated regaled bloated pilloried

8. Don't tell me the whole story; just give me the . . . . of it.
gist gird cede butte

9. The old gentleman had had a few drinks and was quite . . . .
prefatory punitive inebriated irrefutable

10. Some mental disorders are undoubtedly of . . . . origin.
extremist deciduous somatic amenable

11. . . . . trees lose their leaves in the fall.
deciduous supercilious sporadic finite

12. I . . . . you to help me.
assuage enunciate requite entreat

13. Over the years there has been a mass . . . . to the suburbs.
fiasco exodus lope augury

14. This idea will save us a lot of money if it is . . . .
pejorative practicable definitive obsolescent

15. She will receive her Ph.D. degree when she completes her . . . .
provocation introspective dissertation interim

16. We prayed for those unfortunates caught up in the . . . . of war.
pillory amity gamut cataclysm

17. Medical students learn anatomy by dissecting a . . . .
limbo cadaver gamut homily

18. I was horrified to hear him deliver such a(n) . . . . speech.
obsolescent vitriolic bloated disheveled

19. We must . . . . ourselves for the coming battle.
pacify alloy gird anneal

20. He's a real . . . . , always imagining he has some new disease.
martinet hypochondriac pedagogue somnambulist

WORDLY WISE 23

BIANNUAL means "occurring twice a year." *Biennial* means "occurring every two years." Be careful not to confuse these two terms.

DEFINITIVE means "conclusive; final." *Definite* means "clearly defined; precise." A *definite* statement is clear as to its meaning; a *definitive* statement is one that is conclusive and wraps up the subject.

DISCREET means "cautious and tactful" (a *discreet* manner). This word is pronounced the same as *discrete*, which means "separate; detached from each other" (*discrete* particles).

INTIMATE is pronounced *IN-tᵊmit* when it is an adjective (an *intimate* relationship) or a noun. (She told only a few *intimates*.) It is pronounced *IN-tᵊ-mate* when it is a verb. (Did he *intimate* to you what he wanted?)

A STALACTITE is a calcium carbonate formation that hangs down like an icicle in limestone caves. A *stalagmite* is a similar formation that rises up from the ground. Sometimes the two meet and form a column. If these two terms confuse you, think of the *c* in *ceiling* and *stalactite* and the *g* in *ground* and *stalagmite.*

Etymology

Study the roots and prefixes given below, together with the English words derived from them. Capitalized words are those given in the Word List. You should look up in a dictionary any words that are unfamiliar to you.

Prefixes: *extro-* (outward) Latin — Example: *EXTRO*VERT

(Review) *intro-* (inward) Latin — Examples: *intro*vert, *intro*spective

Roots: *chrono* (time) Greek — Examples: *CHRONO*METER, syn*chron*ize, *chron*ic

(Review) *metr* (measure) Greek — Examples: CHRONO*METER*, *metr*ical, *metr*onome

(Review *vert* (turn) Latin — EXTRO-*VERT*, intro*vert*, re*vert*

Word List 24

ASSONANCE	EUPHONIOUS	PECUNIARY
BUTTRESS	FLUSTER	PLEBEIAN
CONCEPTION	GRUESOME	PROCRASTINATE
DIATRIBE	INVOKE	ROUÉ
DISMEMBER	NUTRIMENT	TORSO
ETHNIC		

Look up the words above in your dictionary. Note that many of them have more than one meaning. When you think that you know *all* the meanings of *all* the words, go on to the exercise below.

EXERCISE 24A

From the four choices following each phrase or sentence, you are to circle the letter preceding the one that is closest in meaning to the italicized word. Where the same word appears more than once, you should note that it is being used in different senses.

1. *assonance* in poetry
   (a) nonsense words (b) similarity in vowel sounds (c) imitation of sounds by words (d) harsh, grating sounds

2. a stone *buttress*
   (a) arched bridge (b) supporting structure (c) tombstone (d) round tower

3. to *buttress* an argument
   (a) strengthen (b) refute (c) attack (d) defend

4. to have some *conception*
   (a) swelling of body tissue (b) general idea (c) share in an undertaking (d) hidden purpose

5. the time of *conception*
   (a) the falling of leaves in autumn (b) the earliest period in history (c) extreme old age (d) the beginning of pregnancy

6. a long *diatribe*
   (a) introduction to a book or speech (b) message in code (c) bitterly abusive speech (d) morally uplifting talk

7. to *dismember* it
   (a) forget (b) cut up (c) reject (d) piece together

8. *ethnic* groups
   (a) racial (b) religious (c) political (d) of differing sizes

9. a *euphonious* line of poetry
   (a) incomprehensible (b) pleasant sounding (c) discordant (d) extremely long

10. to *fluster* someone
    (a) seek out (b) confuse (c) suspect (d) amaze

11. a *gruesome* sight
    (a) spectacular (b) horrible (c) appetizing (d) welcome

12. to *invoke* a deity
    (a) act so as to anger (b) request help from (c) no longer believe in (d) curse

13. to *invoke* evil spirits

(a) believe in (b) anger (c) call forth
(d) deny the existence of

14. a lack of *nutriment*
    (a) personal freedom (b) nourishing substance (c) parental control (d) personal discipline

15. a *pecuniary* interest
    (a) financial (b) odd (c) lasting (d) slight

16. *plebeian* tastes
    (a) exotic (b) commonplace (c) cultivated
    (d) hard to please

17. You should not *procrastinate*.
    (a) delay (b) quarrel (c) lie (d) use bad language

18. He is a *roué*.
    (a) member of a secret society (b) leader of people (c) member of the lower classes (d) person who leads a dissipated life

19. a sculptured *torso*
    (a) body minus arms and legs (b) head and shoulders (c) group of figures (d) hand or arm

Check your answers against the correct ones given below. The answers are not in order; this is to prevent your eye from catching sight of the correct answers before you have had a chance to do the exercise on your own.

6c. 11b. 9b. 15a. 4b. 18d. 14b. 1b. 5d. 17a. 2b. 7b. 13c. 10b. 8a. 12b. 19a. 16b. 3a.

Look up in your dictionary all the words for which you gave incorrect answers. Only when you have done this should you go on to the next exercise.

EXERCISE 24B
Each word in Word List 24 is used several times in the following sentences to illustrate different meanings or usage. One of the sentences for each word uses the italicized word incorrectly. You are to circle the letter preceding the sentence.

1. (a) Notice the *assonance* in the words "later" and "paper." (b) The *assonance* of the colors in this painting is particularly striking. (c) *Assonance* is sometimes employed at the end of a line to give a partial rhyme.

2. (a) Large stone *buttresses* at each corner support the walls of the church. (b) The *buttress* of this argument is that too much money is being spent on the project. (c) He had at his fingertips numerous facts with which to *buttress* his argument.

3. (a) The company was granted a *conception* to look for minerals in the area. (b) The *conception* of the plan was entirely hers, but we worked together on its development. (c) From *conception* to birth in humans is a period of nine months. (d) You have no *conception* of the risks involved in a project of this scale.

4. (a) We chose to walk out rather than listen to his *diatribe* against the president. (b) They *diatribed* their political opponents as traitors. (c) She delivered a stinging *diatribe* accusing us of neglecting our responsibilities.

5. (a) He was *dismembered* from the society for giving away its secrets. (b) The murderer had *dismembered* the corpse. (c) The *dismemberment* of the Roman Empire quickly followed the fall of Rome.

6. (a) About half the people were *ethnic* and half were native-born. (b) The people of Hawaii form many different *ethnic* groups. (c) This organization promotes *ethnic* and cultural ties between nations.

7. (a) Telephone operators are chosen for their good manners and *euphonious* voices. (b) The poetry is extremely *euphonious* and demands to be read aloud. (c) The scenery is very *euphonious* in these parts. (d) The melophone, or harmonium is one of the most *euphonious* of musical instruments.

8. (a) He is a calm person, not easily *flustered*. (b) Bees *flustered* around their hives in great swarms. (c) She became *flustered* when she was asked what she had in her shopping bag. (d) Take your time answering their questions and don't let them *fluster* you.

9. (a) The wrecked car with its four mangled bodies was a *gruesome* sight. (b) The newspapers like to *gruesome* a story up to sell more copies. (c) Newspapers compete with each other to give readers all the *gruesome* details of a murder.

10. (a) Her cruel remarks *invoked* me into telling her exactly what I thought of her. (b) The political scientist *invokes* the aid of all the social sciences. (c) He muttered the magic spell that was supposed to *invoke* the spirits of their ancestors. (d) When her personal safety was threatened, she decided it was time to *invoke* the law.

11. (a) In voyages to the distant planets, all necessary *nutriments* will have to be produced inside the spaceship. (b) A balanced diet must include a variety of carefully chosen *nutriments*. (c) She planted a row of *nutriments* next to the peas.

12. (a) As night falls, the bat, the owl, and other *pecuniary* creatures come out. (b) The reward for this work is emotional and spiritual rather than *pecuniary*. (c) Congressmen and congresswomen should declare whether they have any *pecuniary* interest in the awarding of government contracts.

13. (a) A group of *plebeians* had gathered outside the Roman forum to hear the senator. (b) I thought it very *plebeian* of them to serve the food on paper plates. (c) She tried to *plebeian* the people into voting for her proposals. (d) Such vulgar movies have appeal only to the *plebeian* minds of the masses.

14. (a) The longer we *procrastinate*, the more the work will pile up. (b) He is the most *procrastinate* person I have ever met. (c) She should answer the letters, but she *procrastinates*, saying she'll do it later. (d) *Procrastination* is the thief of time.

15. (a) You will *roué* the day that you crossed my path. (b) She called him an old *roué* and refused to have anything to do with him. (c) The old *roué* repented of his misspent life as he lay on his deathbed.

16. (a) He wanted to be admired for his well-muscled *torso*. (b) They *torsoed* their muscles before the race. (c) She is working on a *torso* done in the style of early Greek sculpture.

EXERCISE 24C

This exercise combines synonyms and antonyms. You are to underline the word which is *either* most similar in meaning *or* most nearly opposite in meaning to the CAPITALIZED word. Underline only one word for each question after deciding that it is *either* an antonym *or* a synonym, and write A (for antonym) or S (for synonym) after the capitalized word. Allow only fifteen minutes for this test. If you cannot answer a question, go on to the next one without delay. If you have time left over at the end, go back and try to fill in unanswered questions.

26 or over correct:	excellent
22 to 25 correct:	good
21 or under correct:	thorough review of **A** exercises indicated

1. BODILY .....
   intimate discreet plebeian somatic torso

2. ANNOUNCE .....
   herald invoke palpitate requite entreat

3. RAKE .....
   plebeian torso diatribe roué apologist

4. GRANT .....
   enunciate cede requite perpetrate decry

5. HARANGUE .....
diatribe guillotine fluster alloy telepathy

6. RANGE .....
butte pillory limbo gird gamut

7. RED-FACED .....
affluent inebriated extremist discreet florid

8. DELAY .....
devise pecuniary procrastinate revoke regale

9. SUGGEST .....
enunciate lope perpetrate regale intimate

10. CORROBORATE .....
franchise dismember discredit jettison exonerate

11. IDEA .....
dossier conception provocation pedagogue cataclysm

12. ARRIVAL .....
flux survey affluent exodus interim

13. DISCORDANT .....
euphonious extinct supercilious luminous unremitting

14. PENURIOUS .....
gruesome euphonious bloated sanctimonious affluent

15. TIMEPIECE .....
hypochondriac automaton chronometer fiasco somnambulist

16. PROVOKE .....
demote desiccate germinate buttress pacify

17. SUPPORT .....
oblivion buttress torso gamut emancipate

18. THROB .....
revoke lope palpitate florid prate

19. GRANT .....
revoke invoke disparage assuage herald

20. ARISTOCRATIC .....
hindmost plebeian deciduous extinct ocular

21. BELITTLE .....
default palpitate enunciate disparage entreat

22. CONFUSE .....
fluster buttress invoke extrovert requite

23. START .....
cede inception prate sojourn presentiment

24. FINAL .....
pejorative tacit definitive autonomous extant

25. HORRIBLE .....
finite extremist dogged gruesome sporadic

26. FOREBODING .....
thermal presentiment assonance conception definitive

27. TACTFUL .....
amenable plebeian gruesome discreet deciduous

28. SPOKEN .....
euphonious ethnic tacit affluent autonomous

29. MONETARY .....
belligerent somatic militant punitive pecuniary

30. REPAY .....
requite diatribe procrastinate discredit pacify

WORDLY WISE 24

CONCEPTION and *concept* have similar meanings and are used interchangeably. Note that *conception* defines the act of forming an idea. (The *conception* of this device was hers, but we worked on the development of it together.) *Concept* is an abstract idea that is formed (the *concept* of one God).

Note that PLEBEIAN is both noun and adjective. (He is a *plebeian*; he has *plebeian* tastes.)

ROUÉ is pronounced *ROO-ay*; do not forget the acute accent (´) over the *e*.

Etymology

Study the following roots and prefixes, together with the English words derived from them. Capitalized words are those given in the Word List. You should look up in a dictionary any words that are unfamiliar to you.

Prefixes: *a-* (to) Latin — Example: *A*SSONANCE (Review) *pro-* (forward) Latin — Example: *PRO*CRASTINATE

Roots: *eu* (well) Greek — Examples: *EU*PHONIOUS, *eu*genics

phon (sound) Greek — Examples: EU*PHON*IOUS, *phon*ograph

son (sound) Latin — Examples: AS*SO*NANCE, *son*orous, con*son*ant

cras (tomorrow) Latin — Example: PRO*CRAS*TINATE

ACROSS

1. no longer existing
3. to beat rapidly
6. red-faced; ruddy
9. to put off taking action; to delay
11. an extremely accurate timepiece
12. a feeling of impending misfortune
15. persistent; stubborn (18)
18. to suggest without openly saying
19. to make calm; to soothe
21. to set forth
24. complete; final
25. causing horror or loathing
26. to cut into pieces
28. a yellowish-brown earth color (18)
31. showing care in what one says or does
33. capable of being put into practice
36. a person who leads a wild, dissipated life
37. coming twice a year
38. one who defends or justifies a policy
40. insulting; disparaging
42. one holding immoderate views
43. a song of joy or of praise (2)
45. one who judges or settles a dispute (13)
46. a hanging, iciclelike limestone formation
47. an utterly ridiculous failure
48. having to do with the races of human beings
49. to give up the ownership of
50. similarity in vowel sounds

DOWN

1. pleasant sounding
2. beginning; start
3. concerned with or inflicting punishment
4. having to do with the common people
5. the human body minus the arms and legs
7. a place or condition of oblivion
8. anger; wrath (5)
10. agreeable to being directed; responsive
13. chosen by vote (1)
14. to move at an easy running pace
15. shedding leaves annually
16. to throw doubt on; to disgrace
17. a bitterly abusive speech
20. to make or become confused
22. a substance that nourishes
23. to try to lower in esteem; to belittle
25. to encircle or fasten, as with a belt
27. one whose thoughts are directed outward
29. to give back in return; to pay back
30. to be guilty of
32. an idea or general notion
33. having to do with money; financial
34. a sign foretelling future events (21)
35. a self-regulating machine; a robot
37. a structure that supports a wall
39. of or relating to the body
41. to call forth; to request help from
44. the important part; the essentials

99

Chapter Nine

Word List 25

ABSOLUTE	FLOE	PIED
ATTUNE	HALLUCINATION	RETROSPECTIVE
CENSOR	IMMUTABLE	SEDITION
COVEY	INCANDESCENT	SUCCUMB
EMOTE	LASSITUDE	TENET
FASTIDIOUS	MUNIFICENT	

Look up the words above in your dictionary. Note that many of them have more than one meaning. When you think that you know *all* the meanings of *all* the words, go on to the exercise below.

EXERCISE 25A

From the four choices following each phrase or sentence, you are to circle the letter preceding the one that is closest in meaning to the italicized word. Where the same word appears more than once, you should note that it is being used in different senses.

1. an *absolute* ruler
   (a) wicked (b) operating under the law (c) elective (d) operating without restrictions

2. an *absolute* certainty
   (a) definite (b) qualified (c) stated (d) generally accepted

3. *absolute* alcohol
   (a) frozen (b) pure (c) grain (d) poisonous

4. *absolute* silence
   (a) permanent (b) short-lived (c) complete (d) intermittent

5. to *attune* ourselves
   (a) assert (b) bring into agreement (c) attempt to understand (d) fool

6. to appoint a *censor*
   (a) official who collects taxes (b) official who looks for objectionable material in what is written or produced (c) official who listens to citizens' complaints (d) official who represents his or her country abroad

7. a *covey* of birds
   (a) flock (b) nesting place (c) wire enclosure (d) watcher

8. to watch someone *emote*
   (a) act without using words (b) attempt to conceal emotion (c) imitate the actions of another (d) express emotions dramatically

9. a *fastidious* person
   (a) mournful (b) difficult to please (c) about whom little is known (d) eager to please

10. to keep a lookout for *floes*
    (a) fish that swim with the current (b) logs that float just underwater (c) small sailboats (d) large floating sheets of ice

11. It was a *hallucination*.
    (a) sight existing only in the mind (b) act deliberately intended to provoke (c) sign of the presence of God (d) remark that was unfair and untrue

12. *immutable* laws
    (a) ancient (b) human-made (c) unchanging (d) undemocratic

13. an *incandescent* lamp
    (a) oil burning (b) with adjustable levels of light (c) highly polished (d) glowing with intense heat

14. *incandescent* writing
    (a) insulting (b) brilliant (c) obscure (d) obscene

15. a feeling of *lassitude*
    (a) hunger (b) weariness (c) horror (d) joy

16. a *munificent* reward

(a) given by the city (b) paltry (c) unclaimed (d) generous

17. a *pied* coat
    (a) drab (b) multi-colored (c) close-fitting (d) hooded

18. a *retrospective* exhibition
    (a) wide ranging (b) looking back on the past (c) concerned with the present (d) looking forward to the future

19. acts of *sedition*
    (a) mercy (b) rebelliousness (c) cruelty (d) destructiveness

20. to *succumb* to something
    (a) come close (b) give in (c) object (d) go back

21. Over half *succumbed.*
    (a) died (b) answered (c) lied (d) returned

22. a major *tenet*
    (a) cause (b) principle (c) disaster (d) part

Check your answers against the correct ones given below. The answers are not in order; this is to prevent your eye from catching sight of the correct answers before you have had a chance to do the exercise on your own.

6b. 13d. 11a. 18b. 7a. 17b. 1d. 15b. 22b. 10d. 14b. 9b. 21a. 4c. 2a. 12c. 19b. 5b. 16d. 3b. 20b. 8d.

Look up in your dictionary all the words for which you gave incorrect answers. Only when you have done this should you go on to the next exercise.

EXERCISE 25B

Each word in Word List 25 is used several times in the following sentences to illustrate different meanings or usage. One of the sentences for each word uses the italicized word incorrectly. You are to circle the letter preceding the sentence.

1. (a) Stalin was the *absolute* ruler of Russia until his death in 1953. (b) *Absolute* zero (-459.69°F) is the temperature at which molecules cease all movement. (c) The two men *absoluted* themselves of any involvement in the crime. (d) Are you *absolutely* sure that you paid her?

2. (a) The music he composes is perfectly *attuned* to life today. (b) I asked her to accept the position, and she *attuned* at once. (c) Their minds are not yet fully *attuned* to these modern methods.

3. (a) I could *censor* that something was wrong. (b) Letters from soldiers at the front must be *censored* to ensure that they don't give away military secrets. (c) All plays and movies must be passed by the *censor* before being shown. (d) She's a very *censorious* person, always criticizing others.

4. (a) The fox eluded the hounds and returned safely to its *covey*. (b) A *covey* of partridges suddenly broke from cover. (c) I saw him leave the hotel with a *covey* of his friends.

5. (a) It's fun watching the old-time Hollywood stars *emote* in the silent movies. (b) She *emoted* her lines with great feeling. (c) The actors need to show more restraint; they *emote* in a very exaggerated manner.

6. (a) He is a stylish and *fastidious* dresser. (b) This work requires a *fastidious* attention to detail. (c) That was a most *fastidious* coat you wore yesterday. (d) These furnishings will make even the most *fastidious* families happy.

7. (a) The water continued to *floe* until it froze over. (b) Ice *floes* are a danger to ships in these northern waters. (c) The *floes* break off the ice pack and float south into warmer waters.

8. (a) With many "Goodbyes," "Au revoirs," and other *hallucinations*, they rode off. (b) He

thinks he saw his father, but it was a *hallucination*. (c) During the fever she had *hallucinations* in which she conversed with people from the past. (d) Drugs such as mescaline cause *hallucinations* in those who take them.

9. (a) That matter cannot be created or destroyed was regarded as an *immutable* law of the universe. (b) The old man remained *immutable* for hours at a time, staring silently out of the window.

10. (a) The symphony ends with a truly *incandescent* display of musical fireworks. (b) She's a very *incandescent* girl and won highest marks in her class for three years in a row. (c) The *incandescent* lamp contains a metal filament that glows with great intensity.

11. (a) The *lassitude* of the ship can be determined from the position of the stars. (b) Overcome with *lassitude*, they sank onto the mossy bank and slept. (c) This hot, humid weather causes a general *lassitude* in people, so that very little work gets done.

12. (a) She was awarded the *munificent* sum of half a million dollars. (b) He was a tall, beautifully dressed man with a *munificent* moustache. (c) She received fifty dollars, which seemed a *munificent sum* to one as poor as she.

13. (a) The people speak a kind of *pied* English which is difficult to understand. (b) The *Pied* Piper of Hamelin wore a suit of many colors. (c) The *pied* plumage of tropical birds is certainly eye-catching.

14. (a) In *retrospect*, things don't seem quite as bad as they did when they happened. (b) The workers will get a pay raise of fifty cents an hour *retrospective* to last January. (c) In a *retrospective* mood, she talked of her early struggles. (d) A *retrospective* exhibition puts on display past works of an artist.

15. (a) After the *sedition* is allowed to settle, the clear liquid may be poured off the top. (b) King George III sent an army to deal with his *seditious* subjects in the American colonies. (c) She was jailed for making *seditious* statements. (d) The man who had incited the soldiers to rebel was charged with *sedition*.

16. (a) We *succumbed* that we would not be needed, so we left. (b) She *succumbed* to temptation and opened the package. (c) After a long struggle against the disease, she finally *succumbed*. (d) Many of the nation's banks *succumbed* during the depression of the 1930s.

17. (a) Belief in the divinity of Christ is a major *tenet* of Christianity. (b) It goes against his *tenet* to lend money to anyone. (c) The two great *tenets* of science are observation and deduction.

EXERCISE 25C

The word *rabbit* denotes a burrowing rodent of the hare family with soft fur, long ears, and with the young born without fur.

What might the word *rabbit* connote to the following?

1. a young child who is given such an animal at Easter . . . .

2. a woman who had expected a mink coat and receives instead a coat made out of this animal's fur . . . .

3. a man lost in the forest and dying of hunger . . . .

4. a boxer who is jeeringly compared to this animal . . . .

WORDLY WISE 25

CENSOR and *censer* are homonyms. See Lesson 11 for an explanation of these two terms.

Etymology

Study the following roots and prefixes, together with the English words derived from them. Capitalized words are those given in the Word List. You should look up in a dictionary any words that are unfamiliar to you.

Prefixes: (Review) *retro-* (backward) Latin — Example: *RETRO*SPECTIVE
(Review) *im-* (not) Latin — Example: *IM*MUTABLE

Roots: (Review) *spec* (see) Latin — Examples: RETRO*SPEC*TIVE, *spec*tacle, pro*spect*
muta (change) Latin — Examples: IM-*MUTA*BLE, trans*mute*, *muta*te

Word List 26

ALTRUISM	GIBBET	PROWESS
BOURGEOIS	HIERARCHY	RUSSET
CONFLUENCE	IMPOLITIC	SPATE
DEFICIT	INVALID	SUFFRAGE
ENTAIL	MALCONTENT	THESPIAN
FATUOUS	NATURALIST	

Look up the words above in your dictionary. Note that many of them have more than one meaning. When you think that you know *all* the meanings of *all* the words, go on to the exercise below.

EXERCISE 26A

From the four choices following each phrase or sentence, you are to circle the letter preceding the one that is closest in meaning to the italicized word. Where the same word appears more than once, you should note that it is being used in different senses.

1. to show *altruism*
   (a) unselfish concern for others (b) evidence of improvement (c) selfish concern for oneself (d) evidence of deterioration

2. *bourgeois* tastes
   (a) highly cultivated (b) exotic (c) respectably middle-class (d) scarcely developed

3. the *confluence* of two rivers
   (a) common source (b) coming together (c) effect on the climate (d) combined length

4. a great *confluence*
   (a) crowd (b) event (c) sigh (d) power

5. a small *deficit*
   (a) tax on manufactured goods (b) amount of money short (c) monthly or yearly payment (d) amount of money remaining

6. to *entail* a lot of work
   (a) avoid (b) perform tirelessly (c) make necessary (d) assign

7. to *entail* property
   (a) divide among one's heirs (b) sell at public auction (c) restrict the sale of (d) develop

8. a *fatuous* remark
   (a) helpful (b) foolish (c) wise (d) offensive

9. a *gibbet* at the crossroads
   (a) signpost (b) inn (c) gallows (d) highwayman

10. a religious *hierarchy*
    (a) leader of the highest rank (b) grouping in order of rank (c) objection to what is morally wrong (d) set of rules or beliefs

11. an *impolitic* speech
    (a) impassioned (b) cautious (c) nonpolitical (d) unwise

12. declared *invalid*
    (a) before a court of law (b) of unsound mind (c) before witnesses (d) without legal force

13. an *invalid* person
    (a) wanted (b) tiresome (c) unwell (d) penniless

14. a *malcontent*
    (a) easily satisfied person (b) dissatisfied person (c) person who knows when to stop (d) weak-minded person

15. a *naturalist*
    (a) believer that God is everywhere (b) person who believes all government is undesirable (c) person who studies plants and animals (d) person who refuses the aid of doctors

16. to demonstrate one's *prowess*
    (a) goodwill (b) ignorance (c) ability
    (d) warlike attitude

17. *prowess* in battle
    (a) bravery and skill (b) cowardice (c) cunning
    (d) defeat

18. a *russet* coat
    (a) reddish-brown (b) greenish-blue (c) bluish-purple (d) greenish-yellow

19. a *spate* of books
    (a) large number (b) shortage (c) collection
    (d) history

20. universal *suffrage*
    (a) peace (b) voting rights (c) happiness
    (d) rule of law

21. a famous *thespian*
    (a) actor (b) politician (d) sailor (d) athlete

Check your answers against the correct ones given below. The answers are not in order; this is to prevent your eye from catching sight of the correct answers before you have had a chance to do the exercise on your own.

8b. 12d. 19a. 16c. 3b. 6c. 11d. 21a. 9c. 15c. 4a. 18a. 14b. 1a. 5b. 17a. 2c. 20b. 7c. 13c. 10b.

Look up in your dictionary all the words for which you gave incorrect answers. Only when you have done this should you go on to the next exercise.

EXERCISE 26B

Each word in Word List 26 is used several times in the following sentences to illustrate different meanings or usage. One of the sentences for each word uses the italicized word incorrectly. You are to circle the letter preceding the sentence.

1. (a) It is an *altruism* that you are young only once. (b) In the conflict between selfishness and *altruism*, selfishness usually wins. (c) *Altruism* is one of the basic tenets of the Christian religion. (d) She showed her *altruistic* nature by sharing everything she had.

2. (a) By various tricks he managed to *bourgeois* himself into a position of trust. (b) From her middle-class parents she learned the *bourgeois* virtues of thrift and respectability. (c) After the fall of Napoleon, political power in France fell into the hands of the *bourgeoisie.*

3. (a) The town is located at the *confluence* of the two rivers. (b) The two streams become *confluent* at this point. (c) He was a very *confluent* fellow, able to get along with everyone. (d) At the place where the two roads met, a great *confluence* of people stood waiting.

4. (a) She has a hearing *deficit* that makes it hard for her to hear what is said. (b) The company will operate this year with a *deficit* of fifty thousand dollars. (c) A careful checking of the company books revealed a *deficit* of nine hundred dollars. (d) *Deficit* financing is the raising of government funds by borrowing rather than by taxation.

5. (a) Democracy *entails* a willingness on the part of citizens to take part in political life. (b) She cleaned the chickens and threw away the *entails*. (c) Very little work is *entailed* in this position, and it pays a good salary. (d) Property that is *entailed* stays always within the family and may not be sold.

6. (a) Milk is more *fatuous* from cows that have been fed on fresh grass. (b) It is *fatuous* to argue about it when we don't know all the facts. (c) "Did I do something wrong?" he asked *fatuously*. (d) A *fatuous* grin spread across her face.

7. (a) The bodies of the hanged men were left hanging on the *gibbet* as a warning to others. (b) The condemned woman *gibbeted* with fear as she was led to the scaffold. (c) The highway robbers were *gibbeted* after a short trial.

8. (a) He was the chief *hierarchy* in the Greek church for over twenty years. (b) It takes many years to make one's way to the top of the *hierarchy*. (c) At the bottom of the managerial *hierarchy* are the clerks. (d) The seating arrangement at the banquet was an accurate index of the Hollywood *hierarchy*.

9. (a) It would be *impolitic* to raise the issue at this particular time. (b) A single *impolitic* remark could result in one's being banished from court. (c) They consumed an *impolitic* amount of alcohol and became inebriated.

10. (a) The court declared the document *invalid* because the signature had been forged. (b) She is an *invalid* and spends all her time in a wheelchair. (c) His wounded leg became *invalid* and had to be amputated. (d) That war *invalided* many people.

11. (a) We ignored the grumblings and complaints of the *malcontents* in our midst. (b) They *malcontented* themselves with grumbling and muttering veiled threats. (c) These rumors are started by a group of *malcontent* political outsiders.

12. (a) Earthquakes and floods, unlike wars, have *naturalist* causes. (b) She is a *naturalist* and spends hours in the fields collecting specimens. (c) Carolus Linnaeus (1707-1778) was the great Swedish *naturalist* who set up a classification for plants.

13. (a) The glass case full of cups and medals was evidence of her *prowess* as an athlete. (b) The regiment's *prowess* in battle was legendary. (c) She attempted to *prowess* their guests with an account of Alan's bravery.

14. (a) *Russets* are winter apples with reddish-brown skins. (b) The apples should be picked before they start to *russet*. (c) *Russet* cloth was a brown homespun used by country people. (d) The leaves turn a dried *russet* color in the fall.

15. (a) There has been a *spate* of spy movies in recent years. (b) She is *spated* to attend Friday's meeting. (c) A *spate* of publicity attended the opening.

16. (a) The war caused untold *suffrage* among the common people. (b) *Suffrage* was gradually extended to all persons over eighteen. (c) Women who fought for the right to vote were called *suffragettes*.

17. (a) A company of *thespians* put on a play in the town hall. (b) He developed his *thespian* skills by attending a school for actors. (c) She first learned to *thespian* at the age of four by appearing in plays with her actor parents.

EXERCISE 26C

From the five numbered choices, complete the analogies below by underlining the word that stands in the same relationship to the third word as the second word does to the first. An explanation of analogies is given in the Introduction.

1. scales:weight :: chronometer: (1) space (2) hour (3) measure (4) time (5) distance

2. compound:elements :: alloy: (1) liquids (2) atoms (3) layers (4) metals (5) molecules

3. mental:somatic :: mind: (1) sickness (2) cure (3) physical (4) body (5) thought

4. annual:biannual :: once: (1) double (2) thrice (3) single (4) one (5) twice

5. delicious:taste :: euphonious: (1) harmonious (2) sight (3) sound (4) touch (5) pleasing

6. description:describe :: conception: (1) conceive (2) concept (3) conceptual (4) thought (5) idea

7. pair:two :: covey: (1) bird (2) one (3) flock (4) fly (5) wing

8. wan:white :: florid: (1) red (2) pale (3) blue (4) black (5) green

9. teacher:classroom :: thespian: (1) acting (2) actor (3) play (4) theatre (5) audience

10. aristocratic:aristocrat :: plebeian: (1) upper (2) plebeian (3) vulgar (4) Roman (5) lower

WORDLY WISE 26

BOURGEOIS (pronounced *boor-ZHWA*) is a singular noun (plural *bourgeoisie*) that has the same form as an adjective (*bourgeois* tastes).

GIBBET is pronounced *JIB-it*. The word comes from the Frankish *gibb*, a forked stick.

INVALID is pronounced *IN-və-lid* when it means "unwell"; it is pronounced *in-VAL-id* when it means "without legal force."

Etymology

Study the roots and prefixes given below, together with the English words derived from them. Capitalized words are those given in the Word List. You should look up in a dictionary any words that are unfamiliar to you.

Prefixes: (Review) *im-* (not) Latin – Example: *IM*POLITIC
(Review) *in-* (not) Latin – Example: *IN*VALID

Roots: *mal* (bad) Latin – Examples: *MAL*CONTENT, *mal*ice, *mal*ignant
hieros (sacred) Greek – Examples: *HIER*ARCHY, *hier*oglyphics
archos (ruler) Greek – Examples: HIER*ARCHY*, mon*arch*, olig*archy*

Word List 27

AMORAL	GRIMACE	OUTLANDISH
CARTEL	HUMUS	QUALM
CONUNDRUM	IMPROMPTU	SECULAR
DILEMMA	LARGESSE	SPECULATE
ENUMERATE	MICROCOSM	SURVEILLANCE
FOREGO		

Look up the words above in your dictionary. Note that many of them have more than one mean-

ing. When you think that you know *all* the meanings of *all* the words, go on to the exercise below.

EXERCISE 27A

From the four choices following each phrase or sentence, you are to circle the letter preceding the one that is closest in meaning to the italicized word. Where the same word appears more than once, you should note that it is being used in different senses.

1. an *amoral* person
   (a) in love (b) unconcerned with questions of right and wrong (c) utterly depraved (d) deeply concerned with questions of right and wrong

2. a steel *cartel*
   (a) business firm that has no competition (b) competitive price cutting (c) combine of business firms (d) import tax designed to protect industry

3. a baffling *conundrum*
   (a) performance (b) crime (c) puzzle (d) coded message

4. in a *dilemma*
   (a) state of extreme terror (b) situation involving a difficult choice (c) strange and terrifying situation (d) prolonged and unnatural sleep

5. to *enumerate* his faults
   (a) deny (b) exaggerate (c) list (d) apologize for

6. to *enumerate* the foreign-born
   (a) criticize (b) count (c) separate (d) praise

7. to *forego* something
   (a) look forward to (b) do without (c) lead to (d) cause

8. to *forego* someone
   (a) disappoint (b) precede (c) ignore (d) overlook

9. Don't *grimace*!
   (a) grumble (b) cry out (c) make faces
   (d) dawdle

10. containing *humus*
    (a) heavy concentrations of salt (b) explosive
    or flammable materials (c) diluted alcohol
    (d) decayed vegetable matter

11. an *impromptu* performance
    (a) delayed (b) unrehearsed (c) inept
    (d) polished

12. her *largesse*
    (a) large girth (b) generous gifts (c) talkative
    nature (d) grandiose plans

13. the *microcosm* of the atom
    (a) heavy center (b) destructive power
    (c) unrevealed secrets (d) miniature world

14. *outlandish* clothes
    (a) sturdy (b) peculiar (c) fashionable
    (d) expensive

15. to do it without a *qualm*
    (a) reward (b) pause (c) misgiving (d) plan

16. *secular* music
    (a) ancient (b) modern (c) religious (d) non-
    religious

17. to *speculate* freely
    (a) make demands (b) think reflectively
    (c) voice complaints (d) travel widely

18. to be a *speculator*
    (a) head of a large business firm (b) gambler
    on risky business deals (c) adviser to a govern-
    ment head (d) person who opens up new
    lands

19. under *surveillance*
    (a) observation (b) oath (c) cross-
    examination (d) pressure

Check your answers against the correct ones
given at the top of the page. The answers are
not in order; this is to prevent your eye from
catching sight of the correct answers before you
have had a chance to do the exercise on your own.

8b. 12b. 19a. 16d. 3c. 6b. 11b. 9c. 15c. 4b. 18b.
14b. 1b. 5c. 17b. 2c. 7b. 13d. 10d.

Look up in your dictionary all the words for
which you gave incorrect answers. Only when you
have done this should you go on to the next
exercise.

EXERCISE 27B

Each word in Word List 27 is used several
times in the sentences below to illustrate different
meanings or usage. One of the sentences for each
word uses the italicized word incorrectly. You are
to circle the letter preceding the sentence.

1. (a) A person who would do such a wicked
   thing must have no *amorals* at all. (b) Infants,
   utterly unconcerned with questions of right
   and wrong, are completely *amoral*. (c) Some
   people argue that science is *amoral* and
   cannot tell us how people ought to behave;
   others disagree.

2. (a) *Cartels* have as their purpose the fixing of
   prices and the elimination of competition.
   (b) The companies were accused of trying to
   cartel competition by unfair practices.
   (c) Most countries have now passed laws
   making *cartels* illegal.

3. (a) The answer to the *conundrum* "Why
   didn't the man starve in the desert?" is
   "Because of the sand which is there." (b) How to
   finance the project without raising taxes
   is a *conundrum* no one has been able to
   solve. (c) She was able to *conundrum* her
   questioners with her clever answers.

4. (a) There was no one he could turn to in his
   dilemma. (b) She was in a real *dilemma*; she
   could not help one without hurting the other.
   (c) They didn't know which *dilemma* to
   choose, as both were equally unpleasant.

5. (a) He *enumerated* the advantages of moving

to the country. (b) There was an *enumerate* number of applicants for the position. (c) The population is *enumerated* every twenty years.

6. (a) I must *forego* the pleasure of visiting them. (b) He never *foregoes* an opportunity to remind me of my promise. (c) Our victory was a *foregone* conclusion. (d) You *forego* ahead, and the rest of us will follow.

7. (a) She gave a little *grimace* when told she was going to the dentist. (b) The teacher looked *grimace* when he announced the results of the test. (c) The children *grimaced* when told to eat up all their food.

8. (a) *Humus* the soil into mounds before planting the melons. (b) The more *humus* in the soil, the richer it is.

9. (a) The *impromptu's* job was to remind the actors in case they forgot their lines. (b) He is able to speak *impromptu* and at length on any subject. (c) In an *impromptu* addition to her prepared speech, she thanked her friends for their aid.

10. (a) The young duke headed north, scattering *largesse* at every stopping place. (b) For their support they were entirely dependent on the *largesse* of their grandmother. (c) She brought with her a huge *largesse*, crammed with food and drink of all kinds.

11. (a) A sunken ship is a *microcosm* of the civilization that launched it. (b) The pioneer settlement was a city in *microcosm*. (c) The *microcosm* of a drop of ditchwater yields untold wonders under the microscope. (d) The electrons and *microcosms* in the atom can easily be separated.

12. (a) He spoke *outlandish* to them, but they showed no sign of understanding. (b) They have the most *outlandish* ideas, but occasionally one of them will work. (c) The girl's parents were shocked by the *outlandish* dress of her friends.

13. (a) He had *qualms* about trying to cross the river on such a stormy night. (b) She tried to *qualm* the unreasoning fear that rose within her. (c) He took the money without a *qualm*.

14. (a) She wrote *secular* music as well as hymns. (b) The priestess must *secular* all who come to her in need. (c) Our society is more *secular* than that of a hundred years ago. (d) His parents were opposed to religion and gave their child a *secular* education.

15. (a) She was a tall, *speculate* woman of uncertain age. (b) We must stop this idle *speculation* and find out what actually happened. (c) He *speculated* on real estate during the Florida land boom and made a fortune. (d) It is useless to *speculate* on their fate as we have no information at all.

16. (a) The police kept the woman under constant *surveillance*. (b) The disputed territory is under the *surveillance* of the United Nations. (c) The *surveillance* of the property was approximately twelve acres.

EXERCISE 27C

This exercise combines synonyms and antonyms. You are to underline the word which is *either* most similar in meaning *or* most nearly opposite in meaning to the CAPITALIZED word. Underline only one word for each question after deciding that it is *either* an antonym *or* a synonym, and write A (for antonym) or S (for synonym) after the capitalized word. Allow only fifteen minutes for this test. If you cannot answer a question, go on to the next one without delay. If you have time left over at the end, go back and try to fill in unanswered questions.

26 or over correct:	excellent
22 to 25 correct:	good
21 or under correct:	thorough review of A exercises indicated

1. RUMPLED . . . . .
   fatuous outlandish disheveled munificent pied

2. EXCITING .....
amoral malcontent immutable prosaic retrospective

3. PUZZLE .....
cartel conundrum censor covey microcosm

4. BEG .....
entreat succumb speculate entail emote

5. WEARINESS .....
confluence suffrage assonance provocation lassitude

6. FLOOD .....
spate butte gamut gibbet humus

7. COUNT .....
regale devise enumerate entail spate

8. CONFUSE .....
succumb assuage pillory fluster revoke

9. FLOCK .....
amity covey pillory fiasco limbo

10. PRINCIPLE .....
cartel automaton gamut tacit tenet

11. SURPLUS .....
deficit confluence affluence absolute largesse

12. TOTAL .....
incandescent retrospective absolute secular divers

13. GRATING .....
complacent prosaic supercilious bloated euphonious

14. FOLLOW .....
procrastinate palpitate fluster emote forego

15. CHANGEABLE .....
munificent malcontent invalid immutable impolitic

16. SKILL .....
assonance prowess conception amity gamut

17. SOBER .....
secular russet inebriated absolute fastidious

18. OBSERVATION .....
telepathy surveillance dissertation intimate conception

19. GRANT .....
revoke gird gist discredit buttress

20. GENEROUS .....
munificent altruism fastidious practicable somatic

21. REHEARSED .....
impromptu sporadic autonomous bedeviled dogged

22. START .....
default franchise partiality residue inception

23. FINAL .....
irrefutable obsolescent definitive inevitable desultory

24. SEPARATION .....
provocation inception diatribe cataclysm confluence

25. YIELD .....
devise regale gird succumb requite

26. DISCREET .....
augury impolitic desiccate punitive plebeian

27. ORDINARY .....
introspective desultory complacent outlandish definitive

28. ACTOR .....
courser epaulet thespian covey censor

29. MISGIVING .....
cataclysm qualm amity fiasco torso

30. DELAY .....

disparage   perpetrate   procrastinate   succumb
devise

WORDLY WISE 27

AMORAL is a word believed to have been coined by Robert Louis Stevenson. It means "not concerned with questions of right or wrong." More specifically, it refers to persons or acts that are wicked without there being an awareness of wickedness. *Immoral* means "not conforming to established standards of behavior; wicked and sinful."

A DILEMMA is a situation involving a difficult choice between two alternatives, hence the common expression, "on the horns of a *dilemma.*" A *quandary* is a similar situation, but more serious because the person in it has no idea at all what to do.

FOREGO has two meanings: (1) "to go before; to precede" and (2) "to do without." In this second meaning only, the word is more commonly spelled *forgo*.

LARGESSE is also spelled *largess*.

A MICROCOSM is a world in miniature (the *microcosm* of the atom). This word is contrasted with *macrocosm*, which refers to the universe in its entirety.

Etymology

Study the roots given below, together with the English words derived from them. Capitalized words are those given in the Word List. You should look up in a dictionary any words that are unfamiliar to you.

Roots: *micro* (small) Greek — Examples: *MICRO*COSM, *micro*scope, *micro*meter
macro (large) Greek — Examples: *macro*cosm, *macro*biotics
cosmos (world) Greek — Examples: MICRO*COSM*, *cosm*ic, *cosmo*politan

ACROSS

1. the right to vote in political elections
5. to make risky business deals
12. a sudden anxious or uneasy feeling
13. looking back on the past
14. an expression of displeasure
15. strange; peculiar
17. a large sheet of floating ice
19. a feeling of weariness
22. a scaffold on which bodies were hung
23. a dissatisfied and rebellious person
26. one who studies plants and animals
28. a small group (of birds, people)
29. lacking legal force
31. still in existence (17)
32. glowing with intense white heat
35. decayed vegetable matter
38. a sum of money paid yearly (17)
40. very generous; lavish
42. to show emotion in a dramatic way
43. a large number or amount
44. not concerned with questions of right or wrong
47. unspoken (20)
49. something regarded as a world in miniature
50. an actor
51. great skill or ability
52. an official who examines what is written or filmed for objectionable material
53. to name one by one; to list
54. middle class; smugly respectable

DOWN

1. close observation
2. stupid; foolish
3. perfect; complete; whole
4. to make necessary; to require
6. multicolored; variegated
7. a coming together, as of streams
8. a generous gift; generous giving
9. the condition of being tiresome and wearisome (5)
10. to give way; to yield
11. showing poor judgment; unwise
16. the seeing or hearing of something that is not there
18. a group arranged in order of rank or grade
20. not connected with religion or the church
21. a shortage in the amount of money needed
24. a principle or belief held to be true
25. a difficult choice of two alternatives
27. unselfish concern for others
30. not easy to please
33. an international combine of companies
34. a puzzling problem
36. always the same; unchanging
37. complete absence of law and order (11)
39. without previous preparation or rehearsal
41. a stirring up of rebellion against the state
44. to bring into harmony or agreement
45. reddish-brown
46. to precede; to go before (alternate spelling)
48. a polished face, as of a diamond (3)

Chapter Ten

Word List 28

AGNOSTIC	FINESSE	POTABLE
AMNESTY	GHASTLY	SPINSTER
BAYONET	INADVERTENT	SUBSTANTIATE
DESIGNATE	LISLE	SWATH
EXCAVATE	NOMINAL	TRAVERSE
	PAROXYSM	UNCTUOUS

Look up the words above in your dictionary. Note that many of them have more than one meaning. When you think that you know *all* the meanings of *all* the words, go on to the exercise below.

EXERCISE 28A

From the four choices following each phrase or sentence, you are to circle the letter preceding the one that is closest in meaning to the italicized word. Where the same word appears more than once, you should note that it is being used in different senses.

1. an *agnostic* position
   (a) asserting the existence of God (b) denying the existence of God (c) asserting that the existence of God cannot be known or proven (d) asserting that God and nature are one and the same.

2. granted an *amnesty*
   (a) opportunity (b) audience (c) pardon (d) favor

3. to use a *bayonet*
   (a) spiked ball swung on a chain (b) small fragmentation bomb (c) steel blade that clips onto a rifle (d) long spear with an attached ax head

4. to *designate* someone
   (a) appoint (b) envy (c) scorn (d) abandon

5. to *designate* a place
   (a) design (b) point out (c) bypass (d) leave

6. *designated* as first quality
   (a) passed off (b) described (c) designed (d) sold

7. to *excavate* the ruins
   (a) restore (b) unearth (c) remove (d) search

8. to *excavate* a hole
   (a) fill (b) dig (c) extend (d) cover

9. to show *finesse*
   (a) skill (b) carelessness (c) promptness (d) interest

10. to *finesse* one's way
    (a) know (b) lose (c) trick (d) feel

11. a *ghastly* sight
    (a) supernatural (b) horrible (c) forbidden (d) imagined

12. an *inadvertent* comment
    (a) unnoticed (b) unimportant (c) unintended (d) revealing

13. *lisle* stockings
    (a) silk (b) cotton (c) nylon (d) woolen

14. a *nominal* charge
    (a) fixed (b) variable (c) slight (d) fair

15. a *nominal* ruler
    (a) future (b) holding power by force (c) in name only (d) strong

16. a *paroxysm* of grief
    (a) subdued display (b) holding back (c) sudden outburst (d) polite expression

17. a *potable* liquid
    (a) drinkable (b) poisonous (c) boiling (d) that can be carried

18. *Spinster* is an old-fashioned term.

(a) woman recently married (b) woman whose husband is living (c) woman whose husband is dead (d) woman who remains unmarried

19. to *substantiate* a statement

(a) show to be false (b) agree with (c) show to be true (d) disagree with

20. a wide *swath*

(a) stretch of open water (b) strip of wrapping cloth (c) sweep of a cutting machine (d) sash worn around the waist

21. to *traverse* the region

(a) go around (b) travel over (c) avoid (d) discuss

22. the *traverse* section

(a) that rotates (b) that goes straight up (c) that extends across (d) fixed and immovable

23. an *unctuous* manner

(a) pleasantly at ease (b) showing false concern (c) brisk and efficient (d) showing deep concern

24. an *unctuous* substance

(a) oily (b) evil-smelling (c) medicinal (d) rubbery

Check your answers against the correct ones given below. The answers are not in order; this is to prevent your eye from catching sight of the correct answers before you have had a chance to do the exercise on your own.

5b. 12c. 10c. 17a. 6b. 16c. 1c. 22c. 14c. 21b. 9a. 13b. 8b. 20c. 24a. 2c. 23b. 11b. 18d. 4a. 15c. 3c. 19c. 7b.

Look up in your dictionary all the words for which you gave incorrect answers. Only when you have done this should you go on to the next exercise.

EXERCISE 28B

Each word in Word List 28 is used several times in the sentences below to illustrate different meanings or usage. One of the sentences for each word uses the italicized word incorrectly. You are to circle the letter preceding the sentence.

1. (a) The *agnostic* states that God may or may not exist: we simply do not know. (b) The minister was shocked by the *agnosticism* of his companion on the trip. (c) Her statement that God does not exist is pure *agnostic.*

2. (a) The government granted an *amnesty* to all political prisoners still in jail. (b) She offered to *amnesty* his faults if he promised to mend his ways. (c) The queen promised to *amnesty* all those imprisoned during the civil war.

3. (a) He was invalided out of the army with a *bayonet* wound in the leg. (b) He fired his *bayonet* repeatedly into the ranks of the enemy. (c) They were trained to *bayonet* enemy soldiers without a qualm. (d) The soldiers were ordered to fix *bayonets* and charge.

4. (a) It was necessary for the leader to *designate* a successor. (b) She was one of the *designates* to the first meeting of the assembly. (c) Capital cities are *designated* on the map by circled dots. (d) We will *designate* the three corners of the triangle A, B, and C.

5. (a) Many children were *excavated* to the country during the war to escape the bombing. (b) We struck water as we were *excavating* the basement of the house. (c) Over a million tons of earth were *excavated* to make the tunnel. (d) Great care must be exercised when one is *excavating* ancient ruins.

6. (a) He handles customers with great *finesse* and makes a lot of sales. (b) I admired the

finesse with which the author brought the characters to life. (c) Most of the paintings were *finessed* in different shades of blue. (d) She *finessed* her way into the president's office and explained her idea.

7. (a) The house is haunted by *ghastlies*, and no one goes near it after dark. (b) The battlefield was the scene of many *ghastly* sights. (c) The poor man looked *ghastly* as he was led away after being tortured. (d) Her *ghastly* smile caused us to quake in our shoes.

8. (a) It would be *inadvertent* of you to buy the land as the price is sure to fall. (b) He had *inadvertently* brushed against the painting, smudging it badly. (c) Her failure to answer the last question was due to *inadvertence* on her part and was not deliberate. (d) A single *inadvertent* remark can cause a great deal of trouble.

9. (a) She wore *lisle* stockings to work because they are long wearing. (b) He bought a pair of *lisles* that had been reduced in price. (c) *Lisle* is a hard-wearing cotton fabric used for gloves, stockings, and underwear.

10. (a) There will be a *nominal* charge of fifty cents for the concert tonight. (b) The president is the *nominal* head of state, but the premier wields the power. (c) First, second, third, etc. are called the *nominal* numbers. (d) Because his injuries had been so slight, he was awarded only *nominal* damages.

11. (a) It is a *paroxysm* that truth is stranger than fiction. (b) He doubled up in the *paroxysm* of a racking cough. (c) She flung herself to the floor in a *paroxysm* of grief when she heard the news. (d) He collapsed in a *paroxysm* of laughter when I explained what had really happened.

12. (a) We treated the water with chemicals to make it *potable*. (b) In the box was a *potable* stove that opened up for use. (c) She brought beer, wine, cider, and other *potables*.

13. (a) A woman used to be labeled a *spinster* if she chose not to marry. (b) He had learned to *spinster* wool when he was a little boy. (c) After preparing the flax, the *spinster* sat at her wheel and skillfully began making linen yarn.

14. (a) I can *substantiate* my statement by providing you with proof. (b) Her manner was *substantiate* and inclined to be friendly. (c) No evidence was forthcoming to *substantiate* his claim.

15. (a) *Swath* the baby in blankets to keep it warm. (b) The harvester cut a wide *swath* through the cornfield. (c) She cut quite a *swath* in the business world, becoming a millionaire before she was thirty. (d) By making a wider sweep with the scythe, you can cut a larger *swath*.

16. (a) The drapes are hung from a *traverse* rod and operated by two cords. (b) He was able to *traverse* with the natives in their own language. (c) They reached the lake by evening, having *traversed* the mountain range that morning. (d) The hills are *traversed* by many little mountain streams.

17. (a) Her *unctuous* manner annoyed us because we knew she wasn't sincere. (b) He seemed very *unctuous* to do what he could to help. (c) She makes up large batches of this *unctuous* preparation, which is supposed to be good for muscular aches. (d) "I'm sorry you didn't come in first," said the winner *unctuously* to the runner who had placed second.

EXERCISE 28C

In each of the following sentences a word is omitted. From the four words provided, select the one that best completes the sentence. Allow ten minutes for this test. If you cannot answer a question, go on to the next one without delay. If you have time left over at the end, go back and try to fill in unanswered questions.

18 or over correct: excellent
14 to 17 correct: good
13 or under correct: thorough review of A
exercises indicated

1. We will .... the spot with a cross.
enumerate attune designate perpetrate

2. They bought orange juice, milk, and other ....
conundrums potables amenables practicables

3. They incited rebellion against the king and queen and were charged with ....
sedition largesse suffrage malcontent

4. She should have done this weeks ago, but she loves to ....
diatribe enumerate procrastinate perpetrate

5. That the speed of light is constant is an .... law of nature.
immutable amenable inevitable inebriated

6. He was surprised at being called upon, but gave a charming .... speech.
naturalist pecuniary deciduous impromptu

7. They pitched camp at the .... of the two rivers.
conception covey confluence torso

8. It took us some time to .... ourselves to the new situation.
attune buttress cede forego

9. She fell to the floor in a .... of laughter.
lassitude paroxysm dilemma prowess

10. The job will .... much effort.
succumb invalid enumerate entail

11. A .... charge of twenty-five cents will be made.
deficit nominal retrospective pejorative

12. The government decided to .... the prisoners still in jail.
invoke alloy amnesty augury

13. She received the .... sum of fifty thousand dollars.
munificent luminous obsolescent tacit

14. At the top of the university .... is the president.
cataclysm amity gamut hierarchy

15. Since he receives no money for the work, his interest is obviously not ....
pecuniary introspective supercilious somnambulist

16. She has some strange ideas, but this one is the most .... I have ever heard.
vitriolic prefatory deciduous outlandish

17. Their .... as athletes is not in question.
presentiment deficit largesse prowess

18. .... consists of showing a spirit of generosity to others.
finesse humus altruism sedition

19. Private detectives are keeping the family under ....
amnesty sedition surveillance lassitude

20. The body of the highway robber was left hanging from the ....
gamut gibbet censor punitive

WORDLY WISE 28

An AGNOSTIC is a person who claims that there is insufficient evidence either to believe in or to deny the existence of God. The word was coined by Thomas Huxley (1829–1895), the English biologist and champion of Charles Darwin. An *atheist* is a person who denies the existence of God.

LISLE is pronounced *lile.*

POTABLE means "fit for drinking." *Portable* means "able to be carried."

A SWATH is a band cut by a sweep of a

cutting machine or scythe. *Swathe* is a verb and means "to wrap completely." These two words cannot be used in place of each other.

Etymology

Study the roots and prefixes given below, together with the English words derived from them. Capitalized words are those given in the Word List. You should look up in a dictionary any words that are unfamiliar to you.

Prefixes: (Review) *ex-* (out) Latin – Example: *EX*CAVATE
trans- or *tra-* (across) Latin – Example: *TRA*VERSE

Roots: (Review) *vers* or *vert* (turn) Latin – Examples: TRA*VERSE*, intro*vert*
nomen (name) Latin – Examples: *NOM*INAL, *nom*inate, de*nom*ination
cavus (hollow) Latin – Examples: EX-*CA*VATE, *cav*ity, *cav*e

---

Word List 29

ALLURING	GENRE	SANCTION
ARBITRATE	GHOUL	STARK
BOYCOTT	INTRINSIC	SUCCOR
COLLATE	LYRICAL	TARPAULIN
DIAGNOSE	NUCLEUS	TUNDRA
EXTRANEOUS	PETITION	VERBIAGE

Look up the words above in your dictionary. Note that many of them have more than one meaning. When you think that you know *all* the meanings of *all* the words, go on to the exercise below.

EXERCISE 29A

From the four choices following each phrase or sentence, you are to circle the letter preceding the one that is closest in meaning to the italicized word. Where the same word appears more than once, you should note that it is being used in different senses.

1. an *alluring* prospect
   (a) dubious   (b) complicated   (c) enticing
   (d) limited

2. to *arbitrate* a dispute
   (a) be the cause of (b) deliberately prolong
   (c) aggravate (d) try to settle

3. to *boycott* an organization
   (a) grant an exclusive right to (b) refuse to have dealings with (c) lay criminal charges against (d) form an alliance with

4. to *collate* the texts
   (a) determine the authorship of (b) compare for accuracy (c) make necessary changes in (d) determine the age of

5. to *collate* the pages
   (a) separate (b) put in order (c) correct (d) cut to size

6. to *diagnose* a disease
   (a) take preventive measures against (b) have an unnatural fear of (c) determine the nature of (d) be susceptible to

7. *extraneous* items
   (a) costing a lot of money (b) not really belonging (c) surplus to what is required (d) essential

8. a new *genre*
   (a) discovery   (b) development   (c) kind
   (d) purpose

9. a collector of *genre*
   (a) paintings that depict nature romantically
   (b) paintings that depict gods and goddesses
   (c) paintings that depict everyday life realistically (d) paintings that deal with abstract subjects

10. a young *ghoul*
    (a) person who gets no pleasure out of life
    (b) person who enjoys what most people find unpleasant (c) person who is always in trouble (d) person who says one thing and means another

11. a story about a *ghoul*
    (a) evil spirit that looks like a normal person

(b) evil spirit that robs graves (c) evil spirit that lives on human blood (d) evil spirit that haunts houses

12. the *intrinsic* worth of something
(a) that cannot be calculated (b) placed on a thing by others (c) belonging to the thing itself (d) that is subject to change

13. a *lyrical* account
(a) hard to understand (b) highly detailed (c) emotionally enthusiastic (d) one-sided

14. *lyrical* poetry
(a) humorous (b) songlike (c) dealing with death (d) rhyming

15. the *nucleus* of something
(a) complete collapse (b) central part (c) beginning (d) slow development

16. to prepare a *petition*
(a) solemn, earnest request (b) set of instructions (c) statement of intentions (d) list of requirements

17. to *sanction* its use
(a) question (b) authorize (c) forbid (d) favor

18. to impose *sanctions*
(a) measures to improve trade between nations (b) punitive measures against a nation (c) restrictions on a person's movements (d) limits on the amount that may be spent

19. a *stark* landscape
(a) distant (b) bleak (c) picturesque (d) sunlit

20. *stark* fear
(a) childish (b) needless (c) utter (d) nagging

21. lying *stark*
(a) alone (b) stiff (c) diagonally (d) curled up

22. to *succor* them
(a) aid (b) deceive (c) confuse (d) need

23. a large *tarpaulin*
(a) container for melting tar (b) artist's canvas (c) coal processing plant (d) waterproof canvas covering

24. to cross the *tundra*
(a) dense tropical jungle (b) treeless arctic wasteland (c) lush, fertile valley (d) sheltered inland sea

25. Cut out the *verbiage*.
(a) excess of plants (b) excess of words (c) opening address (d) closing speech

Check your answers against the correct ones given below. The answers are not in order; this is to prevent your eye from catching sight of the correct answers before you have had a chance to do the exercise on your own.

6c. 13c. 11b. 18b. 7b. 17b. 1c. 23d. 15b. 22a. 10b. 14b. 9c. 21b. 4b. 25b. 2d. 24b. 12c. 19b. 5b. 16a. 3b. 20c. 8c.

Look up in your dictionary all the words for which you gave incorrect answers. Only when you have done this should you go on to the next exercise.

EXERCISE 29B
Each word in Word List 29 is used several times in the following sentences to illustrate different meanings or usage. One of the sentences for each word uses the italicized word incorrectly. You are to circle the letter preceding the sentence.

1. (a) Columbus sailed westward, drawn by the *alluring* prospect of discovering an ocean route to Asia. (b) The *allure* of faraway places is a strong one and hard to resist. (c) The fish snapped at the *allure* and found itself being hauled out of the water. (d) She had an *alluring* charm that her friends found irresistible.

2. (a) He offered to *arbitrate* the dispute. (b) The delegates to the convention were chosen in a very *arbitrate* manner. (c) She is a first-class *arbitrator*, often called in to settle

labor disputes. (d) The two parties have agreed to submit their dispute to *arbitration*.

3. (a) The townspeople declared they would *boycott* the store as long as it continued to sell the dangerous toys. (b) The delegates plan to *boycott* the convention unless their proposal is accepted. (c) Over half the members attended the *boycott* that was held last night in the village hall. (d) The *boycott* was successful and normal relations were resumed once more.

4. (a) Promises of help were *collated* from all those interested. (b) My friend *collated* the pages of the magazine, and I stapled them together. (c) The information gathered in the survey is now being *collated*, and a report will be issued soon.

5. (a) The mechanic *diagnosed* and corrected the fault in a matter of minutes. (b) I tried to *diagnose* what she wanted, but with no success. (c) The *diagnosis* shows the patient to be suffering from lung cancer. (d) The doctor *diagnosed* the ailment as a kidney infection.

6. (a) There are a number of *extraneous* incidents in this novel that slow down the action considerably. (b) She is an *extraneous* kind of child with very few close friends. (c) Padded and insulated walls keep out *extraneous* noise while a recording session is in progress.

7. (a) He loves paintings of everyday life and has a fine collection of *genre*. (b) Her *genre* is playing the harp, but she also enjoys the piano and violin. (c) His concerto for strings is a fine example of the *genre*. (d) She writes mainly novels but is interested in other *genres* and has written a few plays.

8. (a) One of Edgar Allan Poe's horror stories deals with *ghouls*, evil spirits that rob graves. (b) The crowd *ghouled* with enjoyment at the scene of the accident. (c) The usual crowd of *ghouls* had gathered to watch the bodies brought out of the wreckage. (d) There is something *ghoulish* in his nature that causes

him to enjoy scenes of misery and misfortune.

9. (a) The puzzle was exceedingly *intrinsic* and took us hours to solve. (b) The *intrinsic* worth of people cannot be measured by their possessions. (c) The *intrinsic* value of the ring was small, but to the person who received it, it was beyond price.

10. (a) The salesperson was positively *lyrical* in praise of the new product. (b) She wrote a number of *lyricals* that were set to music and became popular. (c) The publication of "*Lyrical* Ballads" by Wordsworth and Coleridge in 1798 marked the beginning of the English romantic movement.

11. (a) *Nuclear*-powered ships can travel great distances without refueling. (b) Spokes radiate outward from the *nucleus* of the wheel. (c) All living cells contain a *nucleus* surrounded by a substance called protoplasm. (d) The doctor had a few patients who, she hoped, would form the *nucleus* of a large practice.

12. (a) The Constitution gives the people the right to *petition* the government for redress of grievances. (b) The *petitioners* were led before the king and queen and allowed to make their request. (c) I was asked to sign a *petition* calling for an end to the testing of atomic weapons. (d) The children *petitioned* us to buy them ice cream cones.

13. (a) The plans have received the *sanction* of the mayor and the city council. (b) The church provided a *sanction* for persons wanted by the law. (c) A naval blockade is one of the *sanctions* that may be imposed against a country. (d) The government has *sanctioned* the use of federal funds for low-cost housing.

14. (a) He *starked* back in horror when he saw the snake in front of him. (b) The mountain loomed *starkly* ahead, challenging the climbers to try to conquer it. (c) The body was cold

and *stark*. (d) The *stark* brutality of the prison guards was a great shock to us.

15. (a) Sister Theresa's message was that we must love our fellow humans and *succor* those who need us. (b) The confidence men tried to *succor* him out of his life savings. (c) The shipwrecked sailors received *succor* from the friendly islanders.

16. (a) The *tarpaulined* shelter was quite snug and dry. (b) The road had been recently *tarpaulined* and was still sticky. (c) We threw a *tarpaulin* over the car to protect it.

17. (a) The land had been neglected for so long it had become overgrown with *tundra*. (b) Reindeer eke out a precarious existence on the *tundra*. (c) Only mosses and lichens grow on the treeless wastes of the *tundra*.

18. (a) Buried amid the *verbiage* of her speech was the germ of a good idea. (b) He had planted a few patches of *verbiage* in his little garden.

EXERCISE 29C
Explain the origin of the following words.

1. martinet (Word List 20) . . . .

. . . .

. . . .

2. guillotine (Word List 21) . . . .

. . . .

. . . .

3. thespian (Word List 26) . . . .

. . . .

. . . .

4. bayonet (Word List 28) . . . .

. . . .

. . . .

5. boycott (Word List 29) . . . .

. . . .

. . . .

WORDLY WISE 29
GENRE is pronounced *ZHAWN-rə* .
GHOUL is pronounced *gool*.
LYRICAL is an adjective applied to poetry and means "songlike." *Lyric* has the same meaning in this sense (*lyrical* poetry, *lyric* poetry). *Lyrical* also means "emotionally enthusiastic." (She was *lyrical* in her praise of what you did.) *Lyric* may not be used interchangeably with it in this sense.

Etymology
Study the roots and prefix given below, together with the English words derived from them. Capitalized words are those given in the Word List. You should look up in a dictionary any words that are unfamiliar to you.

Prefix: *col-* (together) Latin — Examples: *COL*LATE, *col*lection
Roots: *verbum* (word) Latin — Examples: *VERBI*AGE, *verb*al, *verba*tim
latus (brought) Latin — Example: COL-*LATE*

Word List 30

AMNESIA	GENUS	SCENARIO
ARBOREAL	HOSTELRY	STINT
BIGOT	LACKEY	SUPPLIANT
CONSTRAIN	MINIMUM	TOOTHSOME
DISPERSE	OBNOXIOUS	ULTRA
FACETIOUS	PLATEAU	VIRTUOSO

Look up the words above in your dictionary. Note that many of them have more than one meaning. When you think that you know *all* the meanings of *all* the words, go on to the following exercise.

From the four choices following each phrase or sentence, you are to circle the letter preceding the one that is closest in meaning to the italicized word. Where the same word appears more than once, you should note that it is being used in different senses.

1. suffering from *amnesia*
   (a) thinness of the blood (b) loss of memory (c) brittleness of the bones (d) spells of giddiness

2. *arboreal* creatures
   (a) tree-dwelling (b) deep sea (c) egg-laying (d) cold-blooded

3. an elderly *bigot*
   (a) fainthearted person (b) narrow-minded, prejudiced person (c) bighearted, generous person (d) important businessperson

4. to *constrain* someone
   (a) restrict (b) encourage (c) insult (d) flatter

5. a *constrained* laugh
   (a) prolonged (b) joyful (c) malicious (d) forced

6. to *disperse* the crowd
   (a) speak to (b) break up (c) win over (d) go with

7. to *disperse* the light
   (a) shield (b) spread (c) reduce (d) shut off

8. a *facetious* remark
   (a) inappropriately funny (b) condescendingly superior (c) angrily scornful (d) deliberately unintelligible

9. a different *genus*
   (a) quality of a person (b) class of living things (c) set of symptoms (d) period in history

10. a large *hostelry*
    (a) inn (b) stable (c) storage bin (d) blacksmith's shop

11. a *lackey* of the governor
    (a) equal (b) companion (c) enemy (d) a servile follower

12. the *minimum* of effort
    (a) scientific measurement (b) smallest amount (c) greatest amount (d) scientific application

13. an *obnoxious* person
    (a) highly dangerous (b) thoroughly unpleasant (c) smooth mannered (d) terribly unlucky

14. an inaccessible *plateau*
    (a) castle in the mountains (b) chain of high, steep mountains (c) broad stretch of high, level land (d) valley surrounded by mountains

15. to reach a *plateau*
    (a) decision either to stop or to continue (b) required level of proficiency (c) place where the road forks (d) temporary halt in progress

16. an exciting *scenario*
    (a) manuscript of a novel (b) script for a stage play (c) motion picture script (d) musical composition

17. without *stint*
    (a) limitation (b) permission (c) care (d) effort

18. a lengthy *stint*
    (a) examination (b) period of work (c) jail term (d) report

19. You will need to *stint*.
    (a) work harder (b) change direction (c) exercise the muscles (d) spend very sparingly

20. the *suppliant* parents
    (a) sturdily independent (b) humbly begging (c) gracefully dancing (d) poverty-stricken

21. a *toothsome* morsel
    (a) brittle (b) tasty (c) tiny (d) poisonous

22. an *ultra* conservative
    (a) extreme (b) old-fashioned (c) new-style
    (d) moderate

23. *ultra*violet
    (a) pale (b) vivid (c) beyond (d) bluish-

24. became a *virtuoso*
    (a) honest and truthful person (b) person who has reached old age (c) believer that humans are basically good (d) skilled musical performer

Check your answers against the correct ones given below. The answers are not in order; this is to prevent your eye from catching sight of the correct answers before you have had a chance to do the exercise on your own.

8a. 12b. 19d. 16c. 3b. 21b. 6b. 11d. 9b. 15d. 4a. 22a. 18b. 14c. 24d. 1b. 5d. 17a. 23c. 2a. 20b. 7b. 13b. 10a.

Look up in your dictionary all the words for which you gave incorrect answers. Only when you have done this should you go on to the next exercise.

EXERCISE 30B
Each word in Word List 30 is used several times in the sentences below to illustrate different meanings or usage. One of the sentences for each word uses the italicized word incorrectly. You are to circle the letter preceding the sentence.

1. (a) The patient was suffering from *amnesia* and could remember nothing. (b) He is an *amnesiac* and has no memory of his life prior to entering the hospital. (c) The government granted an *amnesia* to all political prisoners.

2. (a) The zoo provides trees for its *arboreal* animals. (b) Squirrels build *arboreals* in which to store nuts for the winter.

3. (a) They are *bigots* if they insist that theirs is the only true religion. (b) One of their *bigots* was that the white race is superior to the black and yellow races. (c) She was brought up in a free and open-minded society and had never encountered *bigotry*.

4. (a) He could not be *constrained* to speak against his beliefs. (b) The knowledge that her remarks would be misunderstood *constrained* her from speaking. (c) He threw off the *constrains* of society and went to live on a tropical island.

5. (a) She is not *dispersed* to help you unless you make some effort on your own. (b) A strong wind sprang up and *dispersed* the clouds. (c) The dye is quickly *dispersed* throughout the solution. (d) The angry mob *dispersed* quickly when shots were fired in the air.

6. (a) The *facetious* sides of the diamond sparkled in the light. (b) When the teacher asked who killed Julius Caesar, Billy *facetiously* answered, "Not me, miss." (c) She thought she was being witty when she was merely being *facetious*.

7. (a) The white oak, the red oak, and the English oak belong to the *genus* "Quercus." (b) Horses, asses, and zebras belong to the *genus* "Equus." (c) His application to join the secret *genus* was turned down.

8. (a) She was forced to submit to the good-natured *hostelry* of her classmates. (b) We spent a comfortable night at the *hostelry* and continued our journey in the morning.

9. (a) The great woman's *lackeys* jumped to do her bidding. (b) He was a miserable, *lackey* sort of fellow, with never a kind word to say for anyone. (c) She insisted that she was a devoted public servant and was nobody's *lackey*.

10. (a) He did everything he could to *minimum* the effects of using the low-grade fuel. (b) The *minimum* temperature recorded was -34° F or about -37° C. (c) The cost has been reduced to

121

an absolute *minimum*. (d) The *minimum* wage in the state is determined by the legislature.

11. (a) They were afraid the water might be *obnoxious*, so they boiled it. (b) Our neighbor has the *obnoxious* habit of practicing her trumpet early in the morning. (c) His conclusion that those who disagree with him must be traitors was most *obnoxious*. (d) One of the causes of the American Revolution was Britain's *obnoxious* Stamp Act.

12. (a) The *plateau* region of central Bolivia remains largely unexplored. (b) The surface was *plateau* as a billard table. (c) After making rapid progress at first, students sometimes reach a *plateau* when they seem to be making little, if any, progress.

13. (a) A movie *scenario* is usually the work of a number of people. (b) Excitement is maintained right up to the final *scenario* of the movie. (c) A *scenario* is more commonly called a screenplay.

14. (a) She *stinted* herself on many necessities to buy her ticket home. (b) The United States gave aid without *stint* to Europe in the postwar years. (c) There was a serious *stint* of copper which caused prices to rise sharply. (d) They completed a *stint* in the coal mines before going into business for themselves.

15. (a) The plotters wanted to *suppliant* the king and replace him with his sister. (b) He came to the temple as a *suppliant*, begging for forgiveness of his sins. (c) The *suppliant* townspeople bowed before the conquering army and pleaded with it to spare the city.

16. (a) She felt rather *toothsome* so she bought a bag of almond pastries. (b) Father had made us one of his *toothsome* chocolate cakes.

17. (a) They have an *ultra*modern home, full of the latest appliances. (b) *Ultra*violet rays lie just beyond the violet end of the visible light spectrum. (c) *Ultra* conservatives are fighting to win control of the party. (d) He's very *ultra* and refuses to listen to reasoned arguments.

18. (a) She displayed her *virtuosity* on the violin, the piano, and the cello. (b) He was a child *virtuoso* and performed publicly on the saxophone at the age of five. (c) It was a *virtuoso* performance that brought the audience to its feet. (d) They displayed the Christian *virtuosos* of faith, hope, and charity.

EXERCISE 30C

This exercise combines synonyms and antonyms. You are to underline the word which is *either* most similar in meaning *or* most nearly opposite in meaning to the CAPITALIZED word. Underline only one word for each question after deciding that it is *either* an antonym *or* a synonym, and write A (for antonym) or S (for synonym) after the capitalized word. Allow only fifteen minutes for this test. If you cannot answer a question, go on to the next one without delay. If you have time left over at the end, go back and try to fill in unanswered questions.

26 or over correct:	excellent
22 to 25 correct:	good
21 or under correct:	thorough review of A exercises indicated

1. BLAME .....
   arbitrate constrain succumb exonerate invoke

2. OILY .....
   arboreal facetious unctuous gruesome

3. TASTY .....
   fastidious fatuous munificent potable toothsome

4. USELESS .....
   absolute naturalist definitive extremist practicable

5. PARDON .....
cartel covey amnesty dilemma boycott

6. DIE .....
succumb virtuoso succor spate lope

7. REPUGNANT .....
alluring lackey desultory complacent somatic

8. PALTRY .....
munificent vitriolic obnoxious extraneous immutable

9. INN .....
butte hostelry fiasco limbo boycott

10. APPOINT .....
censor designate entail decry entreat

11. NEAT .....
disheveled munificent retrospective supercilious complacent

12. LIMITATION .....
buttress stint amity augury tenet

13. DRINKABLE .....
affluent fastidious pejorative inebriated potable

14. ENSLAVE .....
boycott disperse emote entail emancipate

15. AUTHORIZE .....
traverse collate sanction devise cede

16. SURPLUS .....
deficit interim amity limbo buttress

17. BURY .....
fluster discredit decry excavate disperse

18. SLOPPY .....
obsolescent fastidious inevitable bloated pecuniary

19. AID .....
covey emote succor alloy devise

20. DELIBERATE .....
inadvertent absolute malcontent fastidious immutable

21. PRAISE .....
cede dismember gird disparage spate

22. CONGREGATE .....
attune censor disperse regale revoke

23. NECESSARY .....
finite extraneous absolute outlandish extinct

24. PLEASANT .....
potable ultra arboreal obnoxious definitive

25. SKILL .....
automaton plebeian finesse fiasco butte

26. SERVANT .....
recluse stint agnostic lackey genus

27. BLEAK .....
finite tacit stint swath stark

28. PLEADING .....
affluent prosaic suppliant supercilious lyrical

29. KIND .....
pied genre gamut qualm prowess

30. RESTRICT .....
succumb entail collate traverse constrain

WORDLY WISE 30

CONSTRAIN is a verb meaning "to restrict"; its noun form is *constraint* (with a final *t*), which means "restriction."

The plural of GENUS is *genera*; *genuses* is also correct. Do not confuse this word with *genius*, a term applied to one of unusually high intelligence. Note that *genus* and *species* (Word List 1) are terms used in classifying kinds of living things; *genus* is the more comprehensive term: a number of different species may form a single *genus*.

ULTRA is an adjective meaning "extreme" (an *ultra* conservative). It is more commonly used as a prefix (*ultra*modern).

Tooth developed the meaning "sense of taste or liking for something" as early as the 14th century. We still use it in this sense when we say that someone has a "sweet tooth." "An eye for color," "an ear for music," and "a nose for news" are similar expressions that use the sense organ itself as a metaphor for ability to perceive. Thus something appealing to the "tooth" is TOOTH-SOME—luscious, or delicious.

Etymology

Study the following roots and prefixes, together with the English words derived from them. Capitalized words are those given in the Word List. You should look up in a dictionary any words that are unfamiliar to you.

Prefixes: (Review) *a-* (without) Greek — Examples: *A*MNESIA, *a*mnesty, *a*theist
ob- (against) Latin — Example: *OB*-NOXIOUS

Roots: *mne* (remember) Greek — Examples: A*MNE*SIA, a*mne*sty, *mne*monics
noxi (harmful) Latin — Examples: OB*NOXI*OUS, *noxi*ous

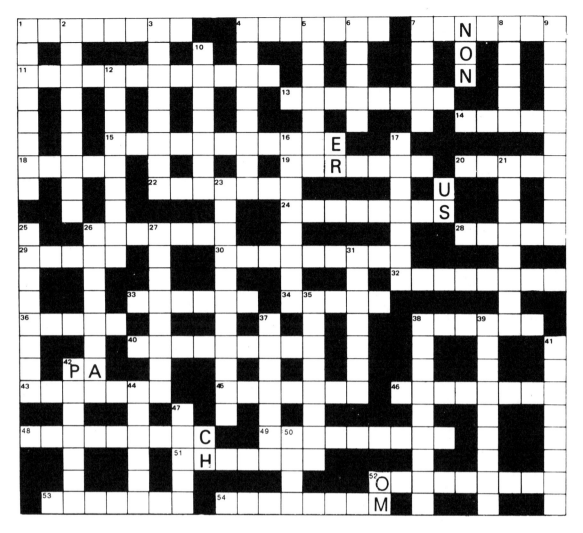

ACROSS

1. to determine the cause or nature of
4. drinkable
7. great skill
11. to show to be true; to verify
13. an excess of words
14. going beyond the usual limits
15. a ruling council of three (12)
18. a strip that is cut or mown
19. emotional and enthusiastic
20. extra-strong cotton thread
22. in name only
24. making a false show of concern
26. partial or total loss of memory
28. a group or class larger than a species
29. a kind or type
30. to give a name to; to call
32. to go across
33. a servile follower; a servant
34. an evil spirit that robs graves
36. bleak; desolate
38. to give badly needed help to
40. joking at an inappropriate time
43. to compare for accuracy
45. a center around which the rest develops
46. a person who spins
48. belonging to a thing in itself
49. a waterproof canvas covering
51. horrible and frightening
52. disgusting; thoroughly unpleasant
53. able to float in water (15)
54. a sudden and violent fit

DOWN

1. to break up; to scatter
2. to intervene in and settle a dispute
3. to authorize or approve
4. a solemn, earnest request
5. a general pardon, especially for political prisoners
6. a place of oblivion (22)
7. to pretend (2)
8. to exercise restraint in spending or giving
9. not really belonging; foreign
10. the smallest amount or degree
12. pleasing to the taste
16. desirable and tempting
17. a steel blade that clips onto a rifle
21. the written script of a motion picture
23. unintentional; not meant
25. neither believing nor disbelieving in God
26. living in trees
27. to take out by digging
31. having to do with water (12)
35. a hotel or lodging place
37. to jointly refuse to have dealings with
38. one who begs humbly
39. to hold back; to check
41. a skilled musical performer
42. a broad stretch of high, level land
44. a vast, treeless arctic wasteland
47. a narrow-minded, prejudiced person
48. pleasingly plump and healthy
50. the second part of four-part harmony (3)